Coaching
the

SOCCER

Coaching tips from the stars

SOCCER

David Scott

*Illustrated by Rodney Paull
and Mike Roberts*

Beaver Books

A Beaver Book
Published by Arrow Books Limited
62–5 Chandos Place, London WC2N 4NW

An imprint of Century Hutchinson Ltd

London Melbourne Sydney Auckland
Johannesburg and agencies throughout the world

First published 1988

Set in Century Schoolbook
by JH Graphics Ltd, Reading

Made and printed in Great Britain
by Anchor Brendon Limited
Tiptree, Essex

ISBN 0 09 961850 8

Contents

The Author expresses his sincerest thanks to all the soccer personalities who have made this book possible through their invaluable contributions. Also, to the following people for their special assistance with the preparation of this book.

Judith Black – Jay Bee Typing Services, Whitley Bay

Reg Corbidge – Sales Director, Newcastle Breweries

John Gibson – Sports Editor, Newcastle *Evening Chronicle*

Malcolm MacDonald

David and Julia McCreery

Bob Moreland – Sports Writer, Newcastle *Evening Chronicle*

Alan Oliver – Sports Writer, Newcastle *Evening Chronicle*

Peter Ratcliffe – Contracts Manager, Dixon Sports

The Directors and Staff of Middlesbrough Football Club

1
The Road to Stardom

The attraction of becoming a professional footballer can be very strong for many youngsters. Dreams of achieving fame, wealth and glory from an enjoyable sport override any thoughts of the pitfalls which might arise along the way. However, any route to the top of such a competitive profession is bound to be long and hard, with many factors, including pure good luck, playing their part.

For most of you, the first step on the ladder will begin at school with selection to the school soccer team, which will usually play competitive or friendly matches against neighbouring schools. Some of the best schoolboys are asked to play for their regional team, and the outstanding young players represent their country at international level. It is a fact that scouts from football clubs go along to many schools, and also to youth matches, in their search for the best young talent in the area.

If you are noticed by a club scout who thinks that you have the exceptional qualities needed to make the grade, the next step is to become an Associated Schoolboy. You can attend the ground for training and coaching sessions and you can play for the club, but only with the written permission of your head teacher. Until the season following your fifteenth birthday, you can play only for the club's team of Associated Schoolboys against similar opposition. You, your parents and your head teacher must sign the Associated Schoolboy forms, after having sought advice from a careers teacher and representatives of the English Schools Football Association. If you become an Associated Schoolboy, the club has an option on your services when you leave school. You must give the club three months' notice prior to leaving school and the club must let you know within fourteen days whether they wish to sign you as a full-time trainee. You are free to sign for another club if you are not offered a traineeship at the club with which you were an Associated Schoolboy.

Until 1987, an apprenticeship system existed which usually lasted for two years from the age of sixteen. An approximate total of 200 youngsters became apprentices each year at the 92 League clubs. Most of our current players came through this very selective system, which offered few educational opportunities. As a result, those who failed to make the grade at eighteen found their job prospects very limited indeed. However, mainly because of pressure from the Footballers' Further Education and Vocational Training Society, there have been some important changes for the better.

All boys entering football from school at sixteen are now registered as football trainees and follow the programme laid down by the Government's Youth Training Scheme. This is a two-year scheme for those who come in at sixteen and a one-year scheme for those who start at the age of seventeen. It involves a day-release course designed by qualified teachers at a college of further education, as well as training in other aspects of football such as groundsmanship and office administration. Many clubs offer even broader areas of work experience, particularly in the leisure industries of sport, travel and tourism. Last year nearly 1200 traineeships were offered to boys, thus benefiting the clubs and giving the trainees far more opportunities than simply those offered through apprenticeships. There are obvious educational benefits in the new scheme, a major step forward in view of the short career which a professional footballer enjoys, and the high failure rate. Only a minority of trainees makes a career in the game, and so it is very important to do well at school and to prepare for a second career while an Associated Schoolboy or trainee.

Even as a professional, you can now successfully continue your education or follow a work-experience course and gain practical qualifications. Grants and advice are given by the Footballers' Further Education and Vocational Training Society, whose Education Officer, Micky Burns, is an ex-professional footballer and schoolteacher.

On the following pages, some well-known professional footballers tell the stories of how they started their chosen careers and who influenced them most in the early days. They also offer some helpful advice to budding pros.

It's a funny game

Len Shackleton, after his six-goal debut for Newcastle in their 13–0 defeat of Newport, said: 'They were lucky to get nil!'

Paul Davis

❝ I was playing for a Sunday side called Tamla
when I was ten years old. At Sunday school I
played for the first team and all my sports
teachers were great influences. I benefited from
the Youth Training Scheme, which gave me the
opportunity to become a professional with
Arsenal, where the back-room staff were
tremendously helpful. ❞

Chris Turner

❝ I started in football by playing for my school
team and then progressing to the City team in
Sheffield. I signed schoolboy forms for Sheffield
Wednesday, who offered me an apprenticeship
and then full professional status. My main
influence was the Sheffield Wednesday and
England goalkeeper Ron Springett. ❞

Steve Clarke

❝ I played football from the age of nine at school
and in youth teams until I was about fifteen. I
then trained with a Scottish junior side called
Beith Juniors. One of their pre-season games was
against St Mirren, who were impressed with my
style of play. They invited me for a week's trial
after which I signed schoolboy forms, and then as
a professional, although only on a part-time
contract. My chief influences were my father and
my first boss at St Mirren, Ricki McFarlane. My
advice to youngsters is to be dedicated to your
football but don't put all your eggs into one

basket. Remember that you may not make the grade for one reason or another and therefore you should try to get a good education. **'**

Brian McClair

' I have played football ever since I could walk. I was lucky enough to be spotted by the scouting system, progressed to an apprenticeship and then on to full professionalism. Everyone I have met in soccer has influenced me in some way, including managers, coaches, players and physiotherapists. You should always work hard, never doubt your ability and listen carefully to advice, especially from more experienced professionals. **'**

John Aldridge

' It was Len Ashurst who signed me for Newport County on the recommendation of his brother, who saw me play for South Liverpool. If you are lucky enough to get the opportunity, make sure you are dedicated and train hard at all aspects of your game. **'**

Peter Davenport

' I played for a local team, then school and representative teams starting with Birkenhead Under-11s. I progressed from there to schoolboy forms with Wrexham and then to Everton as an amateur. In 1982 I signed as a professional for Nottingham Forest, where Brian Clough was a great influence on my career. It is important to choose a club where you respect the manager. Don't get disheartened if things don't always go well for you. You never know what is just around the corner. After all, things may just change for you and then the sky is the limit. **,**

Allan Evans

' Like most players, I started through my school team and was signed as a schoolboy by Dunfermline Athletic, whom I joined as a professional when I left school. I was influenced a lot by Ron Saunders, who brought me to Aston Villa.

Even with the recently introduced trainee system, which gives the opportunity to many more youngsters to make the grade, many clubs are cutting back on the size of their squad because of finances – they simply cannot afford to take on too many players. It is therefore very important to get as good an education as possible before taking up full-time football, because careers are so short and can be affected by injury. For example, as a sixteen-year-old, I broke my leg on my debut for Dunfermline Athletic against Rangers, and that could have ended my career. **,**

Gary Stevens

' From a very young age I can always remember kicking the ball against the side of our house in London. We moved to Suffolk and at eleven years old I started training with Ipswich Town on Thursday nights, with other young hopefuls. I was also playing for my school team and West

Suffolk and Allied Counties Youth League Football, for Bury North End Under-14s.

My father has been the main influence on my career, along with Charlie Woods of Ipswich, Ken Craggs and Alan Mullery, ex-Brighton. Youngsters should enjoy their football, not just the competitive games but also the training. Try to express yourself and you will then entertain the spectators. It is hard work to succeed and nobody sees all that hard work, but you have to put it in. **'**

George Shipley

' I was spotted by a Southampton scout while playing for St Mary's Boys' Club and Newcastle Boys. I was invited down to the Dell for trials and was then signed by Southampton on Associated Schoolboy forms. After many trips down south to train and to play more trial matches, I was then signed on as an apprentice professional when I left school in Newcastle.

My main influences at that time were Jack

Hixon, the Southampton scout who spotted me, and also John McGrath, who was the youth team coach at the Dell. If you ever have the chances which I had, then work hard at training as well as matches, because good habits on the training field will come naturally on the pitch on match day. Always give your best, nobody can ask or expect any more. *Make* things happen and don't just *hope* that they will. A skilful player, with enthusiasm for the game, will have every chance to succeed. One of the first things a manager, coach or scout looks for is enthusiasm. You must show whoever is watching that you have a will to succeed. ❯

Paul McStay

❮ I started playing soccer with a team called Meadonhill United that my father set up in my home town. My father, John, continued to be the main influence in my career. I listen to good advice from anyone, especially people who have been in the game for a long time. ❯

David Armstrong

❮ I was only nine years old when I played for my junior school in Middlesbrough. After signing Associated Schoolboy forms with my home town club, I used to go training at Ayresome Park on two nights a week and during the school holidays. My biggest influence was, and still is, the youth team coach at Middlesbrough, George Wardle. He taught me that self-discipline is the most important kind of discipline to have. ❯

It's a funny game

John Greig, formerly of Glasgow Rangers and known as one of the hardest tacklers in the game, was badly hurt during a particularly tough match. His wife was telephoned by a club official, who broke the news by explaining, 'John is coming home with a broken leg.' She replied, 'Whose is it?'

Martin Foyle

❬ I was spotted playing local football for Bemerton Athletic in Salisbury. From there I had trials with Southampton at the age of seventeen, before signing a one-year apprenticeship at the Dell. My most important early influences were my dad and Ian Branfoot, the Reading manager. It is important for aspiring professional footballers to enjoy the game and not worry about making mistakes. ❭

Kevin McAllister

❬ I used to kick a ball around the streets all day long. Then gradually, when old enough, I played in school and youth teams. My mum and dad influenced me most and gave me the backing and enjoyment, which is important at a young age. My advice is always to have something to fall back on, because injuries or failing to make the grade are so hard to take. Keep your head up and don't lose heart when things don't go right. If you are good enough and have the right attitude, you should come through in the end. ❭

It's a funny game

Jim Pearson, ex-Newcastle United and Everton, once commented upon his exceptional goal-scoring ability: 'I fool the defenders with my pace. I'm deceptively slow!'

Mark Lawrenson

❝ I played for Preston Schoolboys, signed Association forms with Preston North End when I was fifteen and professional forms at the age of seventeen. I come from a footballing family – my father played for Preston and my step-father was a director of the club. From those early days I learned the importance of practice, practice, practice, practice – there is no substitute! ❞

Paul Power

❝ I began at school and played for a Sunday league team. From school, I played for Manchester Boys at under-15 and under-18 level. While playing for these teams, the chief scout of Manchester City Football Club invited me to join the youth teams for training on Tuesdays and Thursdays. From there I progressed into the reserves and then into the first team.

The main influences on my career were my sports-master, Mr Dennis Howells, and the reserve team coach at Manchester City, Dave Ewing, who taught me the basics and good habits. ❞

It should also be remembered that not all professional footballers have followed the same path to the top, some having developed their skills when they were older.

Bob Bolder had a trial with Sheffield Wednesday when he was eighteen-and-a-half years old, and the manager at the time, Len Ashurst, signed him after a week.

Chris Waddle was playing as an amateur for Tow Law in the Northern League and thought his chance of making the top flight had passed by. Chris was spotted by a Newcastle United scout, however, and offered a professional contract.

Cyrille Regis played for Hayes in the Isthmian League until 1977, when West Bromwich Albion paid £10,000 for him. Cyrille was working as an apprentice electrician at the time.

Stuart Pearce started playing for non-League Wealdstone and signed for Coventry from there.

Trevor Peake says, 'I played for non-League Nuneaton Boro' for four years until I was twenty-two, when I signed for Lincoln. I reached the top because I tried my hardest in every possible game, which is the only way to achieve consistency.'

So the message is clear: if you believe that you have the necessary talent but the breaks do not seem to be going your way, then persevere until you do get noticed through sheer hard work, ambition and determination.

2
Player Profile:
Steve McMahon

When all the hard work finally pays off, and a player makes it to the top, it soon becomes obvious that there is still a lot to learn, although the problems may be of a rather different kind. In this chapter one of Liverpool's star players, **Steve McMahon**, reminisces about his first season at England's most successful club, when they won the League and Cup double.

Steve, a former Goodison ball-boy, is one of only a handful of footballers to have played for both Merseyside clubs. It was on 6 September 1985 that Kenny Dalglish paid Aston Villa £350,000 to land this dynamic player. Earlier, Liverpool had wanted to buy McMahon when he was about to leave Everton, but Steve had chosen the Midlands club.

The three years since Steve McMahon's return to his home town, in the first transfer deal of Kenny Dalglish's management, have been by far the most rewarding of his career to date. It was a move which didn't come a day too soon for Steve:

❝ I'd had my opportunity to join the Reds when I left Everton, but it didn't seem advisable to make a cross-city move at the time. I never thought I'd get a second chance, but when I did you can be sure I was never going to mess it up. There was talk of Manchester United wanting to sign me, but all I wanted to do was play for Liverpool. The rumours and the speculations persisted for a month or more, and I was beginning to get really anxious because I'd heard that Villa had rejected Liverpool's first offer. You can imagine how good it felt when I signed along the dotted line. **'**

Steve made his debut at Oxford a week later and, in only his third match, enjoyed a dream return to Goodison Park. Liverpool led Everton by 3–0 at half-time, with Steve blasting home the memorable third goal at the end of a great move that he started himself.

' I'm sure that goal and the fact that we hung on to beat Everton did more than anything to win over the support of any Liverpool fans who had misgivings about the club signing a life-long Blue! It's all about commitment, really. When you show them just how much you want to do well for Liverpool, they soon forget where you came from or what you did before. I don't hear many people refer to me as an ex-Evertonian any more, and that's certainly the way I prefer it. **'**

There were many other golden moments during Steve's first season. He scored in a Milk Cup semi-final, scored twice against Manchester City in the match which took Liverpool to the top of the table for the first time, and figured prominently in the FA Cup semi-final win over Southampton.

⁶ Reaching Wembley on that great afternoon at White Hart Lane represented my happiest memory of all, and yet an injury that I suffered in that match ultimately cost me my place during the run-in to the double.

I didn't notice the pain during the celebrations on the way home, but I wasn't fit enough to figure in the next three matches. As always happens at Liverpool, there is somebody waiting in the wings ready to take their chance, and full marks to Kevin MacDonald, he did it superbly. ⁹

MacDonald kept his place for the last seven games, including the title clincher at Chelsea and the Cup Final against Everton, and Steve was forced to sit out both games as substitute.

⁶ It wasn't the same as playing. I was very sad not to be involved, but those two matches represented the culmination of a season's efforts and there was plenty for me to be proud of.

I didn't really expect to play the way that Kevin was performing. It was a bit like missing out on your own birthday party, but that's life, I have no complaints. It's just made me all the more determined to help get us to the big occasion again. ⁹

Steve learned a lot about the game during his time at the Anfield Academy, although he admits that not once in that time did any member of the coaching staff pull him to one side and tell him how he should play.

❘ They encourage you at different times and in different ways, but they don't dictate to you. Everybody asks you what the Anfield secret is, but it's all down to being businesslike and making no fuss and not complicating things. Mind you, they soon let you know when you are doing something wrong. ❘

The McMahons live in Ainsdale. Like Steve, his wife Julie is a Merseysider and they have two sons, Steve, who is five, and Paul, three.

❘ One or two of the lads used to tease me that I'd never won a medal until I came to Liverpool, and the double maybe meant more to me as a first-timer.

Mind you, I very nearly cost Liverpool the title in 1986. At the start of the season I was playing for Aston Villa against the Reds, in an exciting 2–2 draw. In the last minute I cleared one off the line to deny the lads two points. Imagine if we'd lost the League by two points! ❘

3
Club Coaching Session

Training is essential for any footballer, whether at school or First Division level, and although available facilities may vary it is probably true to say that most amateur teams have access to a local sports centre or school ground that can be used for this purpose. This chapter looks at the way a professional team organizes a training session, and should give you some ideas for exercises you can do at your own local practice centre.

Middlesbrough is typical of many football clubs in that they rarely use their own ground for training, but hire a local sports complex – in this case at Durham University. The facilities there are typical of those needed by a League club and include a sports hall large enough for six-a-side games and general indoor training when the weather is bad, changing rooms, showers and a separate room where the physiotherapist can treat injured players. Outside there are several full-size grass pitches and a hard-surface, all-weather area, which is floodlit.

There is a range of portable apparatus, such as poles, cones and benches which can be used to improve footballers' skills. Simple equipment like these items helps the coach to stimulate interest and vary routines. Cones are very useful for marking out a pitch and altering its shape and size in a matter of seconds. By quartering off the playing area, for example, three or four mini-games can be played. This enables the coach to play small-sided games under realistic conditions. By slotting a pole through the top of a cone, portable goalposts can be made. At least a dozen footballs of the regulation size and weight are available, and allow the coach to get a variety of activities going at the same time.

A section of the field is marked off in 10-metre squares to form a grid, as shown in Figure 1. This can be used to set up practices for shooting, ball control and dribbling.

There is access to a wall, the gable end of the sports hall, which has a paved section in front of it. Every technique can be practised here individually, varying the service by either throwing or kicking a ball against the wall.

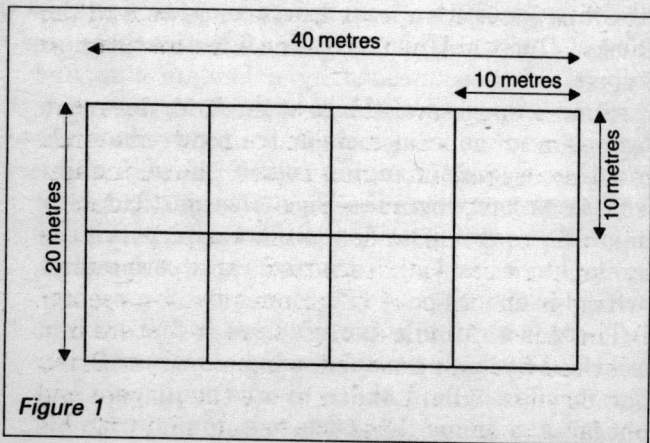

Figure 1

On one particular morning when a Middlesbrough training session was to take place, the weather was dry but icy cold and very windy – a typical winter's day in the North-East. The first to arrive, at 9.30 a.m., was the manager Bruce Rioch, followed shortly afterwards by chief coach Colin Todd and reserve-team coach Brian Little. The session was scheduled for 10.30 a.m. and, with promptness encouraged by late-comers having to pay a fine, the last player was in the changing room by 10.00 a.m. Most of the players had driven the twenty-five miles up the A19 from their Cleveland homes in brand-new sponsored cars, carrying slogans such as 'Bernie Slaven drives . . .', leaving an observer to wonder whether this was a comment on his soccer or motoring skills.

This was going to be a hard session. They'd lost their previous two games and were beginning to slide down the Second Division table. Would this be a typical session? 'Yes,' asserted Bruce Rioch. 'We'll be going for a walk by the river to feed the ducks – that is how Cloughie trains his team at Forest!'

After running several laps of the field, the entire first-team squad was assembled in the centre-circle of the soccer-pitch for what looked like an inquest into their last results. Bruce was gesticulating wildly for over half an hour while the players stood motionless – indeed, frozen to the spot. A spectator arrived in the shape of ITV commentator-presenter Brian Moore. Middlesbrough were to feature in a televised live game the following month, so Brian had flown up from London to see the players and put faces to names. This was to help him with his

It's a funny game

Brian McClair: *During a recent Scotland game, I was sitting on the bench as one of the substitutes. It was only later that I realized that I didn't have any shorts on underneath my track-suit. It's a good job I wasn't needed for the game!*

Steve Clarke: *At Loftus Road, a Chelsea fan removed his clothes, streaked on to the pitch and pretended to score in the QPR net. QPR had the last laugh, however, as Chelsea lost 3–1.*

Bob Bolder: *Most of the funny things tend to happen in training, like the time when Jack Charlton played five-a-side in wellington boots because there was snow on the pitch.*

match commentary – a very professional approach to the job.

In the meantime, the reserves under Brian Little's guidance had started their warm-up routine and it wasn't until they had completed their skills practices that the first team 'inquest' came to an end.

A dozen players were involved in the reserve-team session. Their warm-up consisted of running as a group, twisting and turning as they ran. Short sprints were followed by longer intervals at jogging pace. They stopped periodically for stretching exercises, for example knee mobility, standing on one leg, lifting the other and turning the knee to one side. Players were then organized into two lines and they ran slowly, side by side, together. On a given signal, they darted quickly to the left or right like boxers avoiding punches, before continuing the straight run. To vary the routine, players at the back, on Brian's command, were running to the front of the line, weaving through the players in front of them (Figure 2).

A range of skill practices, shown in Figure 3, was then organized by the coach, and for the rest of the session players moved in rotation to gain experience of each exercise. Brian worked with individuals – coaxing, cajoling, bullying, praising, and constantly reminding players about the importance of good and accurate first-time control in passing.

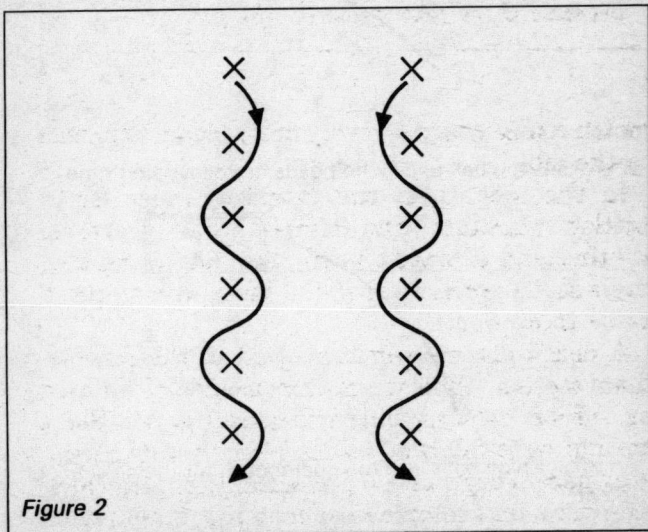

Figure 2

Figure 3

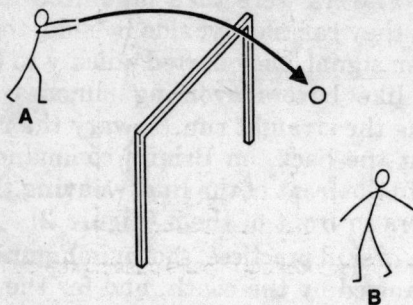

1

A throws the ball over the crossbar to B, who heads it back.

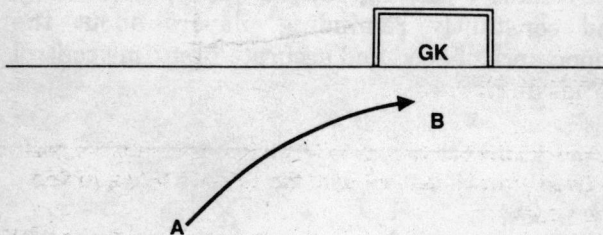

2

A crosses the ball to B, who heads or volleys first time.

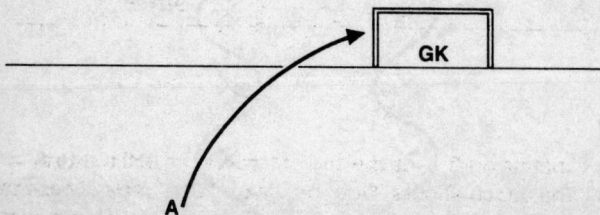

3

A crosses high balls into the goal-mouth for the goalkeeper to catch.

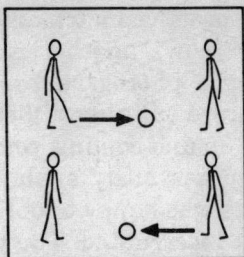

4

In 10-metre grids, working in pairs passing the ball along the ground.

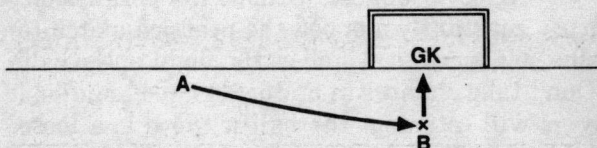

(five-a-side goals)

5

A knocks the ball to **B**, who hits it first time into the goal.

Brian grows impatient with the striker's failure to find the target.

'Watch the ball!' he yells. 'You know where the goal is!'

'Follow through with your foot — don't stab at it!'

6

A variation on 5 — as the server throws the ball out to A^1 or A^2, the coach shouts 'One' or 'Two'. 'One' means pass to the second player to have a shot; 'Two' means have a shot yourself, first time.

Reactions have to be quick — the target must be hit.

At this point, Bruce called for the reserves – he wanted a full-size practice match against his first-team squad. By now, another spectator had arrived, a freelance photographer. A couple of national papers were running a picture story on Bruce Rioch, the up-and-coming young manager. The photographer nervously explained what he wanted, and Bruce was happy to oblige as long as the game was not interrupted. The photographer reminisced about the time he had sat in the bushes at Nottingham Forest's training ground, trying to get pictures of Cloughie without his permission.

Bruce constantly stopped the practice match to get his points across – 'Follow the flight of the ball' – 'Don't take chances in midfield – good midfield players will intercept the ball if there is a loose pass.' He questioned his players: 'How can we keep this game simple?'; 'What other passes could you have made?' He stressed the importance of penetration – getting the ball into the opponents' penalty area as quickly as possible. 'Try it another way, Bernie – it can be done.' Before long, the play was flowing freely and a smile almost began to appear on the manager's face.

4
Advice from Managers and Coaches

While a study of footballing techniques can be very helpful, there is nothing like first-hand experience. In the next two chapters, managers, coaches and players offer their own suggestions on tactics and practice exercises designed to develop overall skill in the game.

Malcolm MacDonald

The most famous names which spring to mind when Newcastle United's past deeds are remembered are Hughie Gallacher, Jackie Milburn and Malcolm MacDonald. The seventies belonged to 'Supermac', as crowds flocked to Tyneside to see this brash, explosive, goal-scoring talent.

Malcolm's interest in soccer began on the terraces of Craven Cottage, watching his Fulham favourites. He played football at school and was picked for the London and Home Counties junior side. At sixteen he played regularly for Knowle Park, and it was with this junior outfit that he first met up with Harry Haslam, who took him to non-League Tonbridge. Haslam moved to Fulham a couple of years later, and Mac unhesitatingly followed him.

It's a funny game

Early in the morning of the day Manchester United played Southampton in the Cup Final, Tommy Docherty wandered down to the barber's shop in the hotel for a shave, and he was charged 50p. On the Monday after the Final, which United lost, he went into a local shop near Old Trafford, to be tidied up again. This time the barber asked him for £3.00. 'Doc' couldn't believe it, and told him that a shave had cost him only 50p in London. 'Ah,' replied the barber, 'but your face is longer today.'

In his first season at Fulham Malcolm, who played at full back, experienced the despair of relegation. In July 1969 he moved to Luton for £17,500, and quickly developed into a natural and prolific goal-scorer. Luton won promotion from the Third Division, with Mac scoring sensational goals along the way. After he had made thirty Second Division goals, Newcastle United manager Joe Harvey paid £180,000 for his services. He arrived at St James's Park in typical style – a chauffeur-driven Rolls Royce. In his League debut at St James's against Liverpool, Mac scored a tremendous hat-trick, which guaranteed him hero-status with the fans. By 1973 Malcolm was a full England international, going on to win fourteen caps including a memorable evening at Wembley, when he scored a record five goals against Cyprus. Malcolm recalls that night vividly:

‘ I was selfish as a striker, and refused to hunt with anybody. After I had knocked the third one in, Keegan came up to me and said, ‘All right, you've got your hat-trick, now how about making one for someone else?’ I replied, abruptly, ‘Get your own.’ ’

One of Mac's greatest disappointments was failing to win a Cup Final medal with United in either 1974 or 1976. When Gordon Lee arrived at the club to replace Joe Harvey, Mac's days there were numbered, mainly because the restrained style of the new manager and the flamboyance of the star were in such stark contrast. Lee's sale of Supermac to Arsenal for £333,333 before the start of the 1976/7 season was a big blow to the St James's faithful supporters. Lee has never been forgiven for selling their idol – the man who had scored 121 goals in a black and white shirt, and the last of the old-fashioned centre-forwards.

After a successful start at Highbury, Malcolm was troubled with a knee injury and operations followed. He was eventually forced to quit the game, later returning to launch a management career with Fulham. This, in turn, was followed by a spell during which he ran a country pub and concentrated upon other business ventures, including a sports agency, which brought the Brazilian international Mirandhina to Newcastle United. Huddersfield Town gave Mac the chance to resume his soccer management career in 1987.

Supermac's advice

Malcolm MacDonald has definite views about goal-scorers:

❛ A goal-scorer is either a hero or a villain, because he will either score or miss. You must appreciate that you have to be the villain some of the time, because to score you must miss – no one is going to take every opportunity that comes during a game. Goal-scorers have to work hard and be the last players off the training field. Be greedy and demand the utmost help from your team-mates. One of the most important things to remember in football is to play to your strengths. My basic strengths were speed, coupled with a good shot and strength on the ball, so I perfected those aspects of my game and eventually, my strengths more than made up for my weaknesses.

Skill practices – set pieces

There is an art to putting the ball in the net from
set pieces – free kicks, corners and throw-ins.
Professionals spend a lot of time in training on
perfecting free-kick moves. You can try the
following ideas with your own team.

Fulham had a lot of success with the exercise in
Figure 4 when I was manager there.
Forward **A** dummies over the ball and makes a
run, wide of the defensive 'wall'. Suddenly, he
stops and walks back towards the ball,
gesticulating at his team-mates around the ball
as if they have caused the move to go wrong. The
wider of the two players on the ball, **B**, then
plays it as shown. Forward **A** spins and runs
behind the wall for the lay-off, making sure that
his timing keeps him on-side for the final pass.

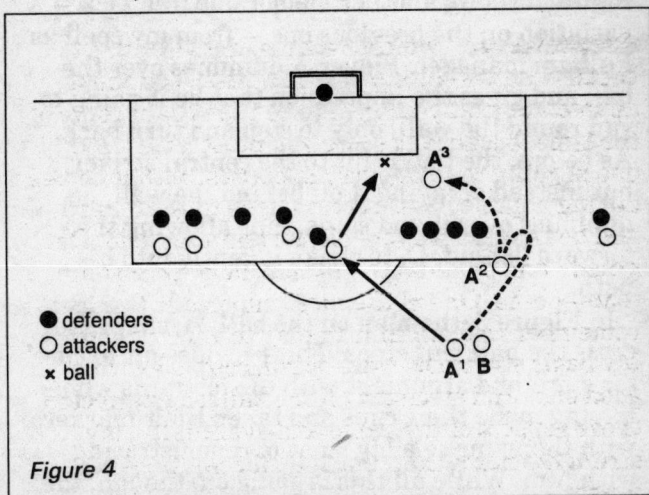

Figure 4

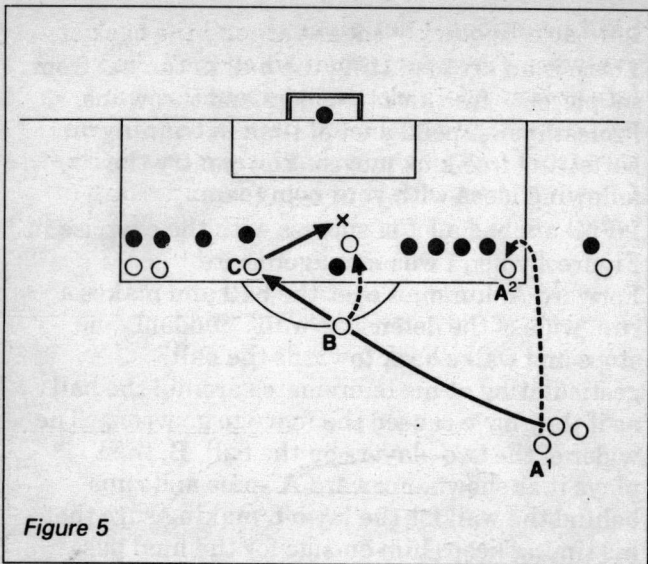

Figure 5

Figure 5 shows another memorable free kick – a
variation on the previous one – from my spell as
Fulham manager. Player **A** dummies over the
ball and gives the impression that he is going to
run round the wall, only to stop and turn back.
As before, the ball is hit to the central striker,
but instead of laying it off behind the wall, he
dummies over it and spins, thus allowing the
forward behind, **C**, to strike it gently into his
path.

In Figure 6, the man on the ball, **A**, shapes to
cross the ball, but stops. This provides an 'excuse'
for a pretend argument with the forwards who,
having made their runs and taken their markers
with them, make a big show of remonstrating
with him. While all this is going on, though, the

36

left-back, **B**, quickly sneaks around the back of everyone. The cross is then hit over all the forwards and defenders and beyond the goalkeeper's reach, the full-back heads it across the face of the goal, and there is the alert striker, **C**, with a great chance to apply the finishing touch.

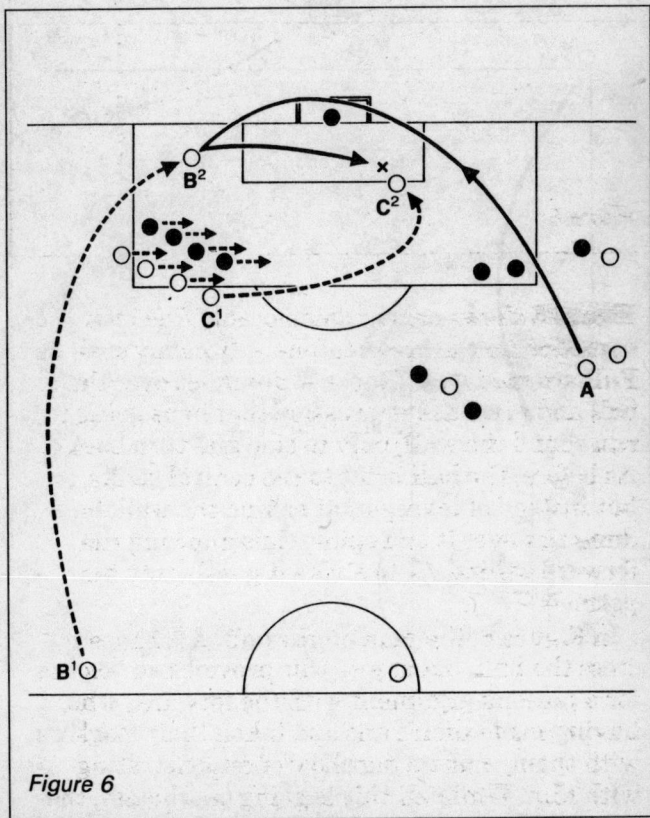

Figure 6

The tactic in Figure 7 is a sort of near-post corner, which you might recall has been used so successfully by the England team in recent years. The ball is played to the near post, where your tallest player, **A**, will flick it on for **B**. Note that the scorer has suddenly come off the line, thus ensuring that he can 'attack' the flick-on properly.

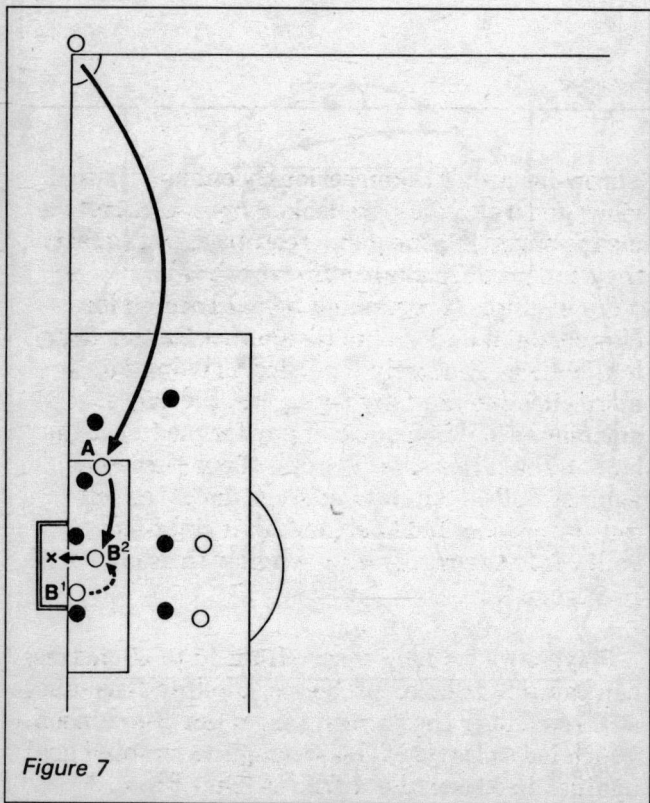

Figure 7

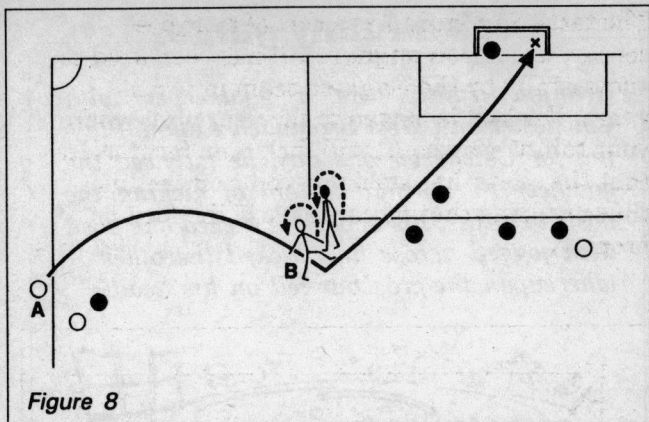

Figure 8

Throw-ins aren't taken seriously enough, in my view; generally they are looked upon as simply a means of getting the game restarted, but in fact they can produce a fair number of goals.

For example, I remember a goal I scored for Newcastle in an FA Cup tie against Bolton. My left foot was generally regarded as being far more effective than my right, and therefore defenders would be quite happy for me to get the ball on the latter side. For one of our throw-ins against Bolton, I dummied to go down the left touch-line, checked back and hit a right-foot volley into the net. I've shown how this happened in Figure 8.

Players with a long throw (from 15 to 20 metres) can cause particular problems. Chelsea fans must still remember the throw-in from Ian Hutchinson, which led to David Webb scoring the winning goal against Leeds in the 1970 FA Cup Final. **9**

Graham Smith was a goalkeeper with Colchester and West Bromwich Albion. Playing for Colchester one day, he followed the goalkeeper's normal custom of kicking the posts to adjust his boots. He kicked one post, then jogged across and kicked the other — whereupon the crossbar fell on his head!

Alex Ferguson

After a successful management career with Glasgow Rangers, Alex moved to England's most famous club, Manchester United. The Scot's most memorable moment was winning the European Cup Winners' Cup against Real Madrid in 1983, making up for the disappointment of losing the Rangers *v* Celtic Scottish Cup Final in 1969.

Alex believes that youngsters who want to reach the top must sacrifice a normal life. His favourite player of all time is Denis Law, who 'epitomized all the ingredients of a top player — skill, enthusiasm and aggression'.

Skill practices

The following practices should be organized in groups of four players.

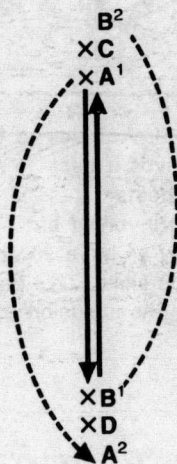

Figure 9

A and B stand approximately 20 metres apart with C and D positioned behind them. A strikes ball with instep to B and runs through. B controls with one touch, if possible, drives ball through to C and runs through. C passes to D and runs through.

These exercises can be repeated with inside of foot or chipping to chest.

Figure 10

A variation of Figure 9. **A** drives to **B** who lays off to
D, gets return and drives it back to **A** who lays off to
C, gets return and repeats.

There is no running involved but you must change
players round, so they all have an opportunity to
develop all the various skills. This particular exercise
can be developed for the inclusion of headers.

It's a funny game

*Stan Cullis, manager of the successful Wolves
side of the 1950s, was giving his players a
roasting after one rare bad performance. He
noticed a smile on the face of the reserve. Cullis
exploded 'I don't know what you're laughing
about, you're not even good enough to get into
the team.'*

Arthur Cox

Arthur prides himself on his discipline and his honest approach to work. He produced one of the most exciting sides of recent years at Newcastle United, where he brought Kevin Keegan and Peter Beardsley to play at front alongside the home-grown Chris Waddle, and then backed them with signings such as Terry McDermott, David McCreery and Glenn Roeder. He left after promotion to the First Division, at the height of his popularity. Arthur took Derby from the Third Division to the First, and then bought England internationals such as Peter Shilton and Mark Wright. He loves good players, and Kevin Keegan was a particular favourite. Speaking of his feelings about the game, Arthur says:

❪ I was encouraged by my parents and at school to play and take part in all sports, and have always enjoyed all kinds of sports ever since. Having tried everything, football is obviously my greatest love. Football now means so much to me and is, in fact, my life.

There is no better profession for any young man to take up, than football. *Don't abuse it!* There are millions who want to be footballers and can't because they don't have the necessary ability, health, etc. If you can play, then make sure that you don't fail. Skill is a very important factor in all sports, but determination and dedication to succeed are also important factors in success, and we have seen skilful players who never reach the top because they lack these two qualities. ❫

Chris Nicholl

In 1985 Chris Nicholl was appointed manager of Southampton, a club where he had earlier enjoyed so many successful seasons as a player. He has now been in the professional game for two decades. However, when he was given a free transfer by Burnley in the mid sixties, he wondered if he would ever make the grade. He went into non-League football with Witton Albion, and made a big impression and was delighted when Halifax Town wanted to sign him. It was only a small club, but it gave him the all-important opportunity of a career in League soccer.

In just over a year with the Halifax side, he did enough to persuade Luton Town to sign him in 1970. Three successful campaigns followed with the Hatters before another move took him to Aston Villa. He joined them at a time when they were trying to clinch promotion from the Third Division. His presence gave them stability in the middle of their defence, and they carried off the Third division Championship in 1972. In 1975, he was in the Villa side which won the League cup at Wembley and secured promotion to the First Division.

He played for six years in the middle of the Saints' defence but was released in 1983, when he started looking around for a coaching or managerial appointment. He went to Grimsby as assistant manager, though he continued to play for two more seasons. When Lawrie McMenemy vacated the managerial chair at the Dell in 1985, Southampton invited Chris to return as boss.

Chris recommends this warm-up routine:

❢ Three teams, each of two to five players in the penalty area extended to sidelines. Each player has a ball. One team tries to 'score', tagging members of the other two teams. Anyone tagged must drop out and squat down by their team-mates touching them. Tagging is done by touching with the hands. If one team succeeds in tagging all the other players, the other team becomes 'tag'. The game ends when all the teams have been 'tag'. ❡

Ray Harford

Ray was coach to John Moore when the latter was manager of Luton. It was one of Ray's first opportunities after an impressive performance during a two-year spell as manager of Fulham under difficult financial circumstances. His talent and belief in attractive play persuaded Luton to make an exception to their usual policy of promotion from within.

Centre-half Ray's professional career took him to half a dozen clubs. He moved to Fulham after coaching Colchester, quickly climbing from youth to first-team coach and then to the manager's chair. Now in the hot seat at Luton, he sees it as the greatest challenge of his career.

Ray advises youngsters to work hard on all skill factors, 'But most of all, obtain good discipline in everything you do, and remember, *practice makes permanent'*.

Billy McNeil

Billy returned to Celtic as manager after spells in England with Manchester City and Aston Villa. He believes that 'youngsters should enjoy the sport and be prepared to "give" to the sport, before looking for anything in return'.

Steve Harrison

Steve was a player at Watford before eventually returning as manager. He stresses the importance of practising the basic skills of passing, chipping, driving and controlling the ball with different parts of the body. 'All practices should be done in a non-competitive atmosphere.' He warns youngsters not to play too many football matches and advises them: 'Listen with respect and then decide which is good or bad advice. Ask questions, go and watch good players and concentrate on watching their every move, rather than the game as a whole.'

John Hollins

John Hollins is, by and large, a one-club man and intensely loyal. He made the journey from playing through coaching to management. John is the model professional, representative of all that is good in football. He had to withstand considerable pressure during his management career at Chelsea before leaving the club in 1988.

He advises youngsters to concentrate on all types of ball control, using knees, feet and head. 'Work hard, train hard, listen to all advice and always give your best.'

John suggests this skill practice, to help you to develop ball control:

❬ In a 10-metre square, by yourself, kick the ball in the air two or three bounces in succession, without using your hand or arm. The ball must not touch the ground and you must remain inside the square all the time. Repeat this, keeping the ball up in the air for as long as possible. Try to improve on your last achievement every time. ❭

It's a funny game

George Shipley: When attempting to take a corner kick, I once kicked the corner flag out of the ground and it spun through the air.

Playing for Reading against Portsmouth, I was hit on the head by a telephone directory when taking a throw-in.

47

Mark Lawrenson

The Preston-born six-footer began his career with Preston North End, switching to Brighton in a £100,000 move after 73 League appearances. He made over 150 appearances with the Sussex club, and helped them gain promotion to the First Division, before going to Anfield for £900,000 in August 1981. Although reckoned to be the most complete defender in Europe, he has won several of his Republic of Ireland caps in midfield. Oxford United gave him his first opportunity in management.

Mark stresses the importance of learning to kick with both feet, and offers the following advice:

6 There are some basic principles to be learned when kicking the ball. If your knee is kept over the ball, it will stay low. It is best to approach the ball at an angle, left or right depending on which foot you're kicking with. Put your knee and head over the ball and kick through; that way you control the power.

To try to get the ball into the air, the head must be back away from the ball. Lean back so that the ball is kicked on the way up. Place the standing foot just behind the ball, where you feel most comfortable. Follow through and allow the natural swing of the foot to send the ball in the right direction. **9**

Practise kicking skills with a partner, as shown in Figure 11.

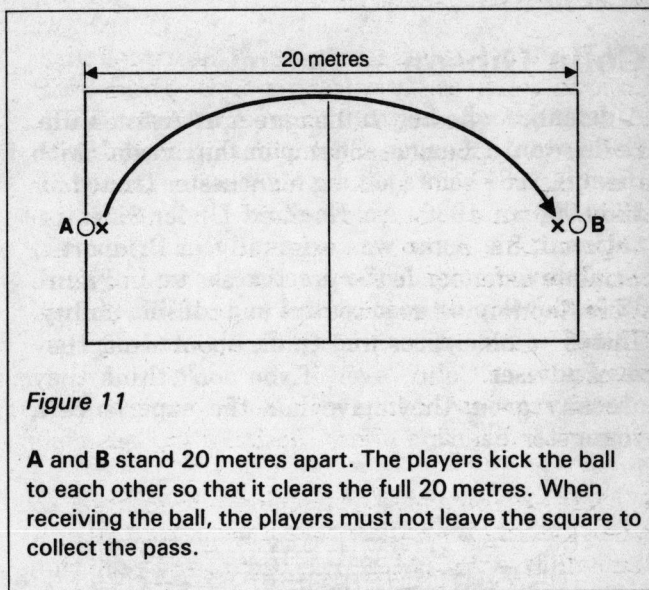

Figure 11

A and **B** stand 20 metres apart. The players kick the ball to each other so that it clears the full 20 metres. When receiving the ball, the players must not leave the square to collect the pass.

5
Advice from Players

We've had some sound words from the managers and coaches – now let's hear from the players themselves.

Colin Gibson – Defender

A defender who began his career at Aston Villa, Colin won a League Championship medal with them in 1981 before joining Manchester United for £250,000 in 1985. An England Under-21 international, his home was originally in Bridport.

Colin recommends the practice shown in Figure 12 for developing good control and passing ability. 'Listen to older pros and think about what they say,' advises Colin, 'even if you don't think they are any good; they have had the experience a youngster hasn't.'

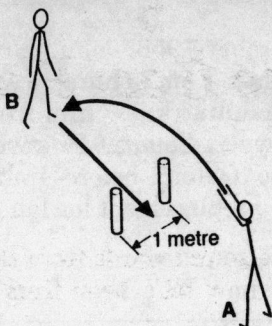

Figure 12

A throws the ball to B standing 5 metres away. B controls
the ball before it touches the ground. Using no more than
two further touches, B must pass the ball back to A so
that the ball passes between the two skittles, situated
1 metre apart.

Peter Davenport – Striker

Peter started his career with Nottingham Forest,
scoring 54 goals in 118 games, before moving to
Old Trafford in March 1986 for £575,000. Peter is
an England international.

❝ It is surprising how many professional footballers cannot kick with both feet. There is nothing
more basic than finding a wall and attempting
to kick a ball backwards and forwards
against it. First try ten shots with your left
foot and then ten with your right. Eventually the
ball will keep coming back to you, and at the same
time you are improving your weak foot and
obtaining a better balance. ❞

51

John Aldridge – Striker

Born 18 September 1958, John nearly signed for Sunderland when Len Ashurst was manager at Roker Park (Ashurst knew him from their days together at Newport County). However, John eventually went to Oxford before linking up with Liverpool as the replacement for Ian Rush. The fee was £750,000.

Shooting practice

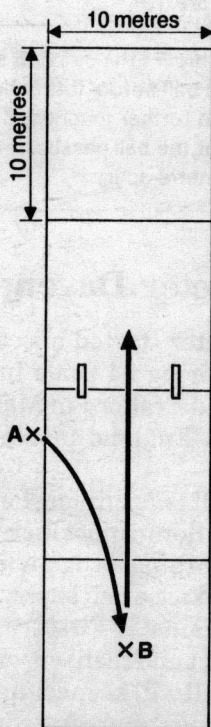

10 metres

10 metres

Figure 13

A throws the ball so that it bounces in **B**'s square. **B** must control the ball first bounce or in the air, and shoot accurately from inside the end square, through the goal using no more than two further touches.

A×

×B

It's a funny game

During a charity cricket match in the 1950s, Frank Brennan, a tall, rugged, fearless centre-half, was at the wicket with his Newcastle United team-mate Jackie Milburn. Milburn stroked the ball to a fielder and set off for a quick run. The fielder reacted quickly and threw the ball high towards the wicket-keeper, at the end to which Brennan was running. Realizing that he was never going to reach the crease in time, big Frank powerfully headed the ball out of the way and completed the run.

Keith Houchen – Striker

Born in Middlesbrough, Keith is a six-foot-plus striker, who has scored 117 goals in 356 matches for Hartlepool United, Orient, York City and Scunthorpe United. Keith signed for Coventry in 1986 for £60,000, and has continued his impressive scoring record at top level. He won an FA Cup Final medal with Coventry City in 1987.

Shooting Practice

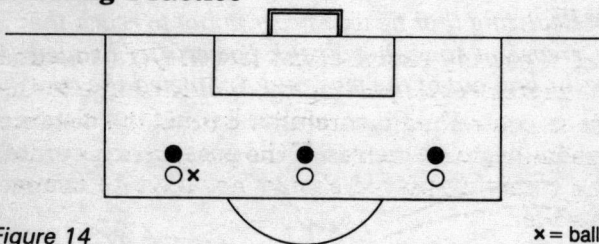

Figure 14   × = ball

Play 3 v 3 in the penalty area with a neutral goalkeeper. One team attacks and tries to score goals, or if in defence, tries to avoid conceding goals. The goalkeeper starts the game by throwing the ball out. The ball is trapped and passed to a team-mate, who must have a shot. Ball possession changes after interceptions, if the ball goes out of play or after a foul. If the goalkeeper gathers the ball, or if it goes over the goal-line, the game is re-started with a throw. The need to shoot frequently and when under pressure is great practice for match situations.

Keith advises: 'Work hard at your goal attempts. It took me ten years in the game, but I eventually played in the greatest spectacle of all – the FA Cup Final.'

Greg Downs – Defender

Born in Nottingham, Greg was signed by Norwich City straight from school. He made his first team debut as a centre-forward but quickly switched to defence, and played 200 games for the Canaries at left back. Coventry signed Greg from the East Anglian club in the summer of 1985. He recommends: 'Listen to advice, but still try to keep your own individuality when playing.'

Skill

For a passing exercise, get two players to stand 10 metres apart, passing the ball from one to the other, controlling it carefully. Extend the distance gradually, to 40 metres. If the passing is accurate, the receiving player should not have to change position.

Steve Gritt – Defender/Midfield

A long-serving Charlton player, Bournemouth-born Steve has played in every position for Athletic, including goalkeeper. Signed from AFC Bournemouth on a free transfer in 1977, he quickly established himself as Charlton's most valuable squad player. Also an accomplished cricketer, Steve has represented Hampshire Second XI. He believes that it is important for a player to build up stamina, and Figure 15 illustrates an exercise designed for this purpose.

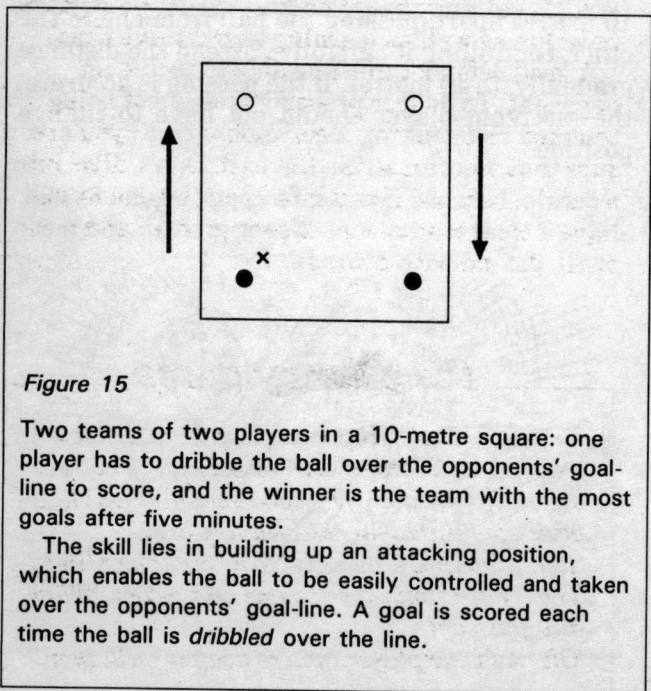

Figure 15

Two teams of two players in a 10-metre square: one player has to dribble the ball over the opponents' goal-line to score, and the winner is the team with the most goals after five minutes.

The skill lies in building up an attacking position, which enables the ball to be easily controlled and taken over the opponents' goal-line. A goal is scored each time the ball is *dribbled* over the line.

Colin Foster – Defender

Colin joined Nottingham Forest from Leyton Orient during the 1986/7 season, following a spell on loan at the City ground. He quickly bridged the gap between the Fourth and First Divisions. In his final match of that season, he scored his first goal for Forest in a 2–1 win over Newcastle United. Colin is a Northern Ireland international.

❝ Let youngsters develop at their own pace and enjoy football. When they reach twelve to fourteen years, then start teaching them basic skills. Training should be fun, so that youngsters have fun as well as learning at the same time.

A good defender must be able to tackle an opponent. To do this properly means not being tempted into making a movement until you are sure that you can strike the ball. Don't 'dive' into a tackle, because if you miss, your opponent will have a clear run to goal. Never give up and most of all, defend with courage. ❞

It's a funny game

During a match between two First Division teams, a well-known and respected referee was shouted at by a player who thought a foul had been committed in the penalty area.

'Ref, that was a penalty. You must be blind.'
The referee stopped the game and asked, 'What did you say?'

'Oh,' said the player, 'you're deaf as well, then.'

Nick Pickering – Midfield

Sunderland snapped up this local youngster, and Nick played 192 senior games for the Wearsiders before Coventry signed him for a fee of £120,000 in January 1986. His League debut was against

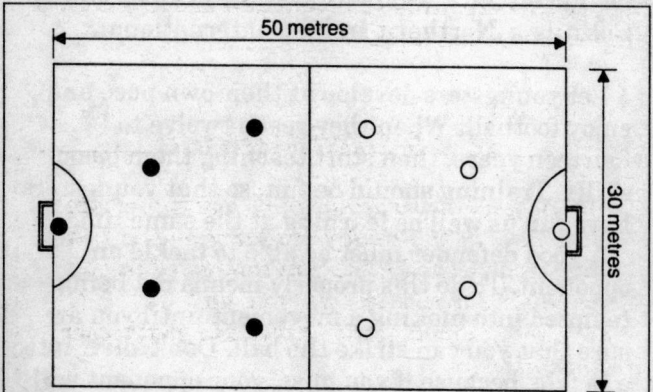

Figure 16

'Conditional' five-a-side games help you to concentrate on a particular aspect of the game. Play to five-a-side rules on a small pitch, but for approximately five minutes during the session, concentrate upon one of the following conditions:

i) A player can touch the ball only twice before passing it. This rule prevents players from holding on to the ball for too long.

ii) No pass should be more than 5 metres — this prevents long, aimless passes.

iii) A player cannot pass the ball back to the player who last touched it. This encourages movement amongst the team.

Newcastle United, his home-town team. An England international, Nick has also won sixteen Under-21 caps.

' Practise hard — do not become disillusioned but always remember that talent on its own is not always sufficient to succeed. A lot of luck is required as regards selection and keeping free of injuries — Good Luck! '

It's a funny game

As the goalkeeper limped off, having let nine past him in a Sunday league game, a little man approached him. 'I'm interested in you,' he said. 'I'd like to sign you up.'
'Are you a talent scout?' asked the goalkeeper, hopefully.
'No, son. I'm an optician.'

Eddie Niedzwiecki – Goalkeeper

Welsh-born Eddie made his name with Wrexham before joining Chelsea for £55,000. A Welsh international, Eddie had established himself as regular number one 'keeper before injury interrupted his career.

Reaction practices

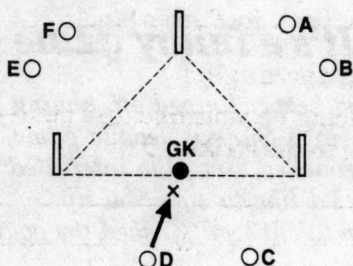

Figure 17

Place three posts in the form of a triangle. Six players, **A–F**, position themselves about 15 metres from the goal, in a circle. The ball is passed between them and shots are taken quickly. The goalkeeper must change his position within the three posts as the position of the ball changes.

Chris Turner – Goalkeeper

A former youth international and Sunderland 'Player of the Year', Chris left Sunderland during the summer of 1985, when his contract expired. He signed for Manchester United at a fee fixed by an independent tribunal at £275,000. Chris must have doubted the wisdom of that move when at first he was very much in reserve at Old Trafford. A group of Sunderland businessmen recently launched an appeal (which eventually failed) to bring Chris back to Sunderland.

Narrowing the angle

❝ By advancing up your line, you cut down the angles open to the striker. ❞

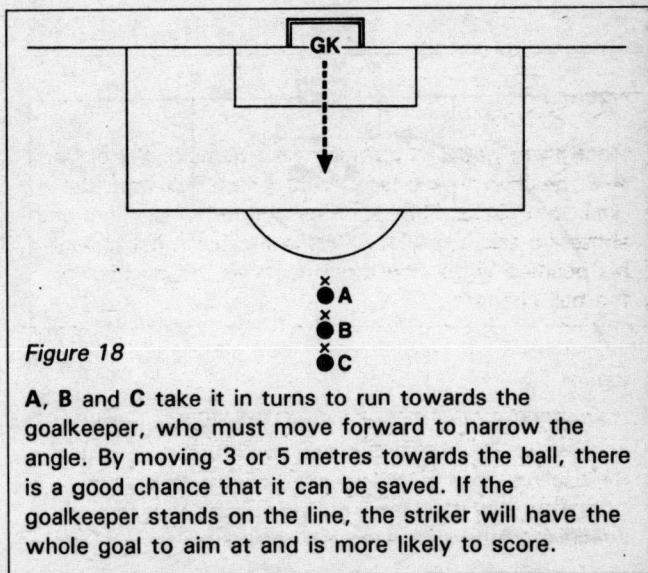

Figure 18

A, B and C take it in turns to run towards the goalkeeper, who must move forward to narrow the angle. By moving 3 or 5 metres towards the ball, there is a good chance that it can be saved. If the goalkeeper stands on the line, the striker will have the whole goal to aim at and is more likely to score.

John Lukic – Goalkeeper

Chesterfield-born John was an England Under-21 international, and joined the staff at Elland Road as a schoolboy, making 146 League appearances for Leeds United before transferring south to Arsenal for £75,000 in 1983.

❢ Goalkeepers should always catch a ball if possible, and then pull it into the chest straight away, so that if challenged they are less likely to lose it. If the ball is just a little bit too far out to catch, then push it clear with one fist or two, to propel the ball as far away as possible from the goal. Punching is usually used only when the goalkeeper is under pressure and might not be able to catch the ball. ❢

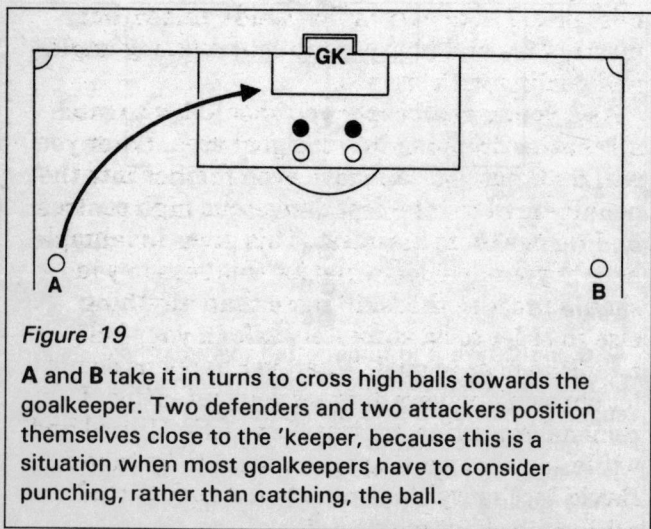

Figure 19

A and **B** take it in turns to cross high balls towards the goalkeeper. Two defenders and two attackers position themselves close to the 'keeper, because this is a situation when most goalkeepers have to consider punching, rather than catching, the ball.

❝ A goalkeeper must make his run early and confidently, concentrating on the flight of the ball. Punch with two fists rather than one, and punch 'through' the ball, not at it. Be prepared to move your own players by your determined run and jump, and always be aggressive. ❞

Neville Southall – Goalkeeper

Neville's distinguished performances in goal for Winsford United put him on the road to success in League football. Bury signed him for £6000 in 1980 and he did enough in one season to persuade Everton to sign him for £150,000. Neville is also first choice 'keeper for Wales.

❝ As a goalkeeper you must keep learning. You must practise the basics but also learn from your mistakes. I take part in five-a-side games, but mostly I try and improve my catching, my angles and dealing with crosses.

As a young goalkeeper you should try to catch all centres dropping into the goal area. Later you will find that you can move even further into the penalty area to intercept dangerous high centres and render them harmless. This gives invaluable help to your defenders and for this reason you should practise this skill more than anything else in order to be absolutely safe in your ball handling near to goal. Whatever happens do not let opposing players distract your attention. I remember playing against Newcastle United and while we were waiting for a corner to be taken, David McCreery stood next to me and started asking me about my dad! ❞

Ray Clemence – Goalkeeper

Ray has been capped by England on 61 occasions. He began his career with humble Scunthorpe United, but Liverpool signed him in 1967 and he enjoyed ten glorious years at Anfield, winning just about every honour available. Ray moved on to Tottenham for £300,000 in 1981. He lists the highlights of his career as winning the 1977 European Cup Final with Liverpool in Rome, and captaining England against Brazil at Wembley.

Catching a high ball

❛ With the high ball, keep both eyes on the ball, use both hands and spread your fingers behind the ball so that it cannot slip through. The goalkeeper's greatest problem is to get the maximum height while holding a balanced position. Jump high, take off on one foot. The stride before you plant your take-off foot is the

It's a funny game

Fred Eyre, an ex-player and now a successful businessman, said that a coach came up to him before one game and said, 'I want you to do a Pacific job for me today.'
Fred replied, 'Well, you'll have to give me oceans of room.'

On a separate occasion, another coach said, 'Fred, I want you to play today like you've never played before. I want you to play well.'

long one which allows you to swing your free leg powerfully forwards and upwards. This free leg swing assists you to gain a greater height.

Try to avoid a situation from which you have to jump from a standing position. If your jump is forwards and upwards, you will gain greater height. **'**

Figure 20

A, the server, lobs ball towards goalkeeper.

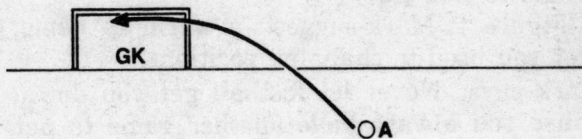

A crosses high balls into the penalty box.

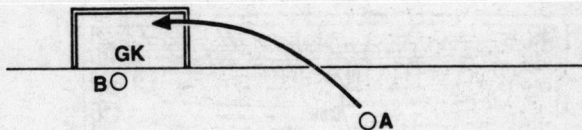

A crosses high balls into penalty box and goalkeeper has to catch the ball under challenge from an opponent (**B**).

Mark Reid – Defender

In the two seasons following Mark's £40,000 transfer from Celtic to Charlton Athletic in May 1985, he remained ever-present in the side, and broke three club records during the course of an unbroken 104-match run. He became Charlton's record penalty scorer in a season when he netted eight times in 1985/6. He was the first player to take three penalties in a match, and finally, in the 1986/7 season, his 57 senior appearances constituted a record in a campaign by a Charlton player.

While at Celtic, Mark was capped by Scotland at Under-17, –18 and –21 levels and picked up quite a collection of club honours, winning two League Championship medals, League Cup winners' and runners-up medals, and a Scottish FA Cup losers' medal in nearly 200 outings for the famous Scottish club.

In Figure 21 Mark suggests a 'warm-up' game, to get you used to changing positions.

Mark says: 'Never let football get you down, because you always have another game to put things right.'

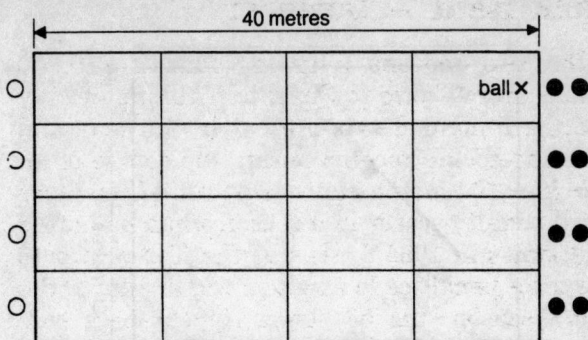

Figure 21

Four teams — three players to a team: one player
stands across the pitch from the two other members of
his team, who have the ball. One of these two passes
the ball across to his team-mate and sprints after it:
the receiver passes the ball back to the third man and
likewise sprints across. A constantly changing position
is thereby achieved. The winning team is that which
completes the greatest number of changes within the
time allowed (either five or ten minutes).

Stuart Pearce – Defender

Stuart soon established himself as a firm favourite
with Nottingham Forest supporters following his
transfer from Coventry City during the summer
of 1985. He maintained high standards throughout
his first season at Forest, and was rewarded when
the England Manager, Bobby Robson, selected him
to play for England against Brazil and then
Scotland.

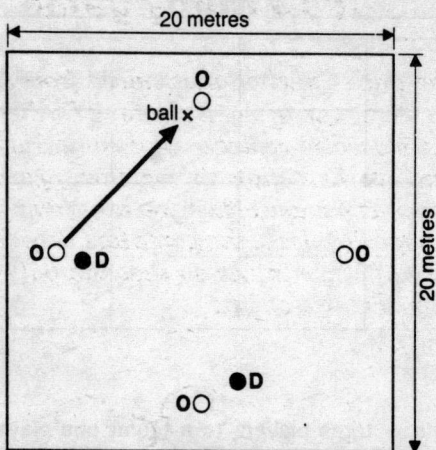

Figure 22

Four against two: the four players (O) must pass the
ball among themselves; the two defenders (D) must try
to intercept their passes by careful positioning. The
sequence is broken only if the defenders touch the ball
or if it goes out of play. In these cases, the player who
last touches the ball changes with one of the
defenders; otherwise, changes can be made on a rota
basis.

Stuart says: 'Remember that running off the ball
is being done correctly when the player with the
ball has three opportunities of passing.'

After Jack Charlton had moved from playing into team management, Tommy Docherty was once moved to remark, as a comment on the speed of the action in matches against his teams: 'You know, when you are playing a side managed by Jack, the game has to be stopped every fifteen minutes so that the ball can be given the kiss of life!'

Mike Duxbury – Midfield/Defender

Mike is a versatile player who has appeared in both defence and midfield over his years with Manchester United. After gaining Under-21 honours, he earned ten full caps for England.

Mike says, 'I joined United straight from school and made my debut against Manchester City. Your debut is always something special, but this was made more so for me because it was a local derby game.'

Soccer marbles

Try the dribbling skills shown in Figure 23. They are important to learn, whatever your position.

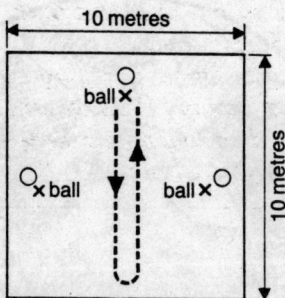

Figure 23

Three players in a 10-metre square. Each player has a ball. One in each square dribbles his ball up and down, the other two try to knock the dribbler's ball away from his feet. A player can kick only his own ball. If a shot misses, the player must get the ball back himself. If he 'scores' he changes places with the dribbler.

It's a funny game

Newcastle manager Gordon Lee once burst into the dressing room after training and asked, 'Is Aidan McCaffrey Irish?'
'No, boss.'
'Are his parents Irish?'
'No, boss.'
'How dare he have a name like McCaffrey and not be Irish?'
Apparently Lee wanted to recommend Aidan for the Eire international squad.
'Steady on, boss,' said 'Supermac', the Newcastle striker, 'my name is Malcolm MacDonald, and you can't get more English than me.'
Lee snapped back, 'You should never be allowed to play for England with a Scottish name like MacDonald.'
By this time the whole dressing room was in hysterics, and Tommy Cassidy sent Lee storming out of the door when he asked, 'Excuse me, boss, but are you Chinese?'

David Armstrong – Midfield

At his peak, David was one of the most accomplished midfield players. Still enjoying his football on the south coast, David can be found in his own penalty box as often as he is attacking that of the opponents. He specializes in left-foot shots from around the 25-metre mark.

71

Shooting

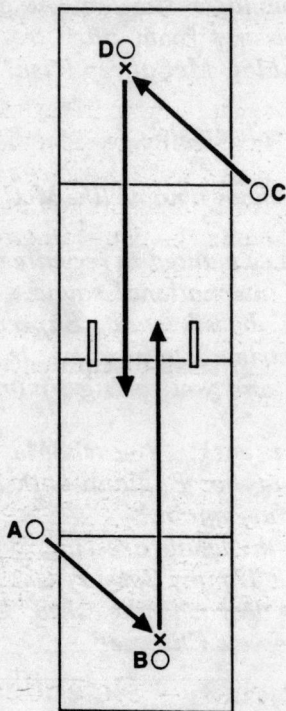

Figure 24

In fours, using 4 squares on the grid. From outside the
grid, **A** rolls a ground pass into **B**'s square. **B** runs forward
to shoot through the goal. He must do so in two touches,
one to control and one to shoot, or if he wishes he may
shoot first time.

The sequence is then repeated by **C** and **D** from the
other end.

David began his career with Middlesbrough, and in one spell made 356 consecutive team appearances. Southampton signed him for £600,000 in 1981, and he has been capped three times for England.

❲ I have been very fortunate in my career, to have played with so many good footballers. The teams I most enjoyed were the Second Division promotion team at Middlesbrough and the host of stars which made up the Southampton team when I first arrived there. ❳

David believes that it is important for youngsters to learn self-discipline, to practise, listen and learn.

Gerry Forrest – Defender

A qualified joiner, do-it-yourself expert and snooker player, North-East-born Gerry was signed by Southampton from Rotherham in December 1985. He had been with Rotherham since the age of twenty as a regular first-team player. Explains Gerry, 'I was playing non-League when Mike Carr, a Rotherham scout, invited me to play a few games for the reserves. I turned professional a couple of months later.'

Gerry got a great thrill out of winning the Third Division Championship with Rotherham in 1981. He advises: 'Try to work a lot on ball skills in training. Once you can control the ball comfortably, you're half-way there.'

Controlling the ball

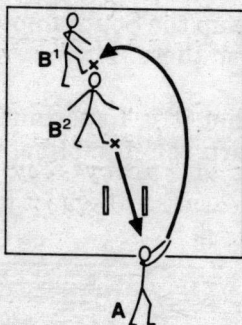

Figure 25

In a 10-metre square, **A** throws to **B**, standing not less than 5 metres away, who controls the ball before it touches the ground. Using no more than two further touches, **B** tries to pass the ball back to **A** so that the ball passes cleanly in between the two skittles, 1 metre apart.

It's a funny game

David Campbell: While leaving the field after a live television match in front of millions of viewers, I tripped over the television cable and fell flat on my face.

Steven Hardwick – Goalkeeper

A former England youth international, Steve began his professional career with Chesterfield before moving to Newcastle United for £100,000 in 1977. He joined Oxford in February 1983 and made 129 consecutive League appearances, helping them to win the Third Division Championship and, later, promotion to the top division. One of Steve's big disappointments was that his parents were unable to witness the Third Division Championship trophy and medals being presented at the Manor Ground.

Steve is also a successful coach, involved with several local teams, and is first to heed his own advice: 'Listen, but don't always copy. In the latter part of my own career, my biggest influence has been Steve Hardwick.'

General advice

❝ Goalkeeping is a very specialized job. It is often said in the game that goalkeepers have to be a bit mad to want to play there. They certainly have to be dedicated. The essentials for goalkeeping are a good pair of hands, courage, being able to work out angles, alertness, anticipation and good reactions. A goalkeeper must be able to direct the play in front of him, tell the defenders where he wants them and who should be marked. A good call will also help to get defenders out of trouble, so that they can run, turn, clear the ball or play it back to the goalkeeper.

An essential technique which needs to be practised is that of *diving, to save low, medium and high balls.* ❞

Diving in pairs

i) Server stands facing the goalkeeper and rolls the ball some 2 to 3 metres to left or right. The goalkeeper dives to hold the ball.

ii) Server throws the ball to the ground so that it bounces no higher than a metre to the left or right. The goalkeeper, from a standing position, pushes off to make a short, low dive and catches the ball as it bounces upwards.

iii) Server, facing the goalkeeper, throws the ball at a steep angle in the direction of one of the uprights. As the ball makes contact with the ground, he flings his body across the space between him and the post, to catch the ball.

iv) Free practice of diving saves; this time the partner shoots towards the goal at varying heights.

David O'Leary – Defender

Born in north London and brought up in Dublin, where he went to secondary school, David (nicknamed 'Spider') was discovered by Arsenal scout Gordon Clark, and taken to Highbury. Having made his League debut as a seventeen-year-old at the start of the 1975/6 season, after one year as an apprentice, David is the Gunners' longest-serving player. Highlights of his career include winning the FA Cup Final and a debut for Eire against England at Wembley. Losing to Valencia on penalties in the European Cup-winners' Cup Final still ranks as his greatest disappointment.

David offers the following advice:

‘ Always try to improve your game, no matter how good you are. From an early age get used to touching the ball with both feet, even if this means just kicking it against a wall. For a defender, it is also very important to learn how to head the ball correctly. ’

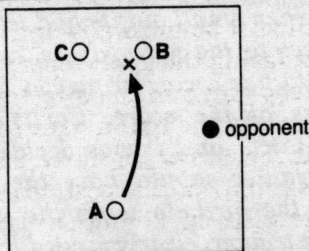

Figure 26

3 v 1 practice with opposition. The server, **A**, about 5 metres from the receiver, serves the ball with an underhand throw to either **B** or **C**, who heads it back to the server. The three then try to make six consecutive passes with their feet without losing the ball to the opponent. When they have done that, or when the opponent gets the ball, the practice is repeated, the ball being served by whoever is in possession. Practice continues until everyone has been both an opponent and a receiver. In the early stages the opponent should be positioned at some distance from the server and the receiver (8 metres), so that the challenge cannot be made too quickly. As heading ability increases, the distance can also be increased.

David says, 'It is important for the player heading the ball to move quickly into a supporting position, so that the consecutive passing movement with the feet can be started successfully.'

It's a funny game

In a chat show on Tyneside, Lawrie McMenemy told the story of an old trainer at Carlisle United many years ago, when the side was playing in a cup competition away from home against a non-League team. It was before the days when small outfits had telephones to relay scores to the newspapers, and so each side had to use a carrier-pigeon to fly home with news of the score. Carlisle won an exciting match, and it was decided that the popular trainer should have the honour of releasing the bird, to wing the great news home. The trainer, clearly excited by the result and the honour bestowed upon him, was given the pigeon, which he lifted to his lips and shouted, 'Tell them we won 3–2!' He then released it into the sky as the club secretary stood speechless, still holding the piece of paper which should have been attached to the pigeon's leg.

Lawrie Madden – Defender

Lawrie began his career as an amateur with Arsenal before graduating from Manchester University. After returning to the South, he established himself with Charlton Athletic before joining Millwall. He was given a free transfer from the Den to join Sheffield Wednesday in 1983.

Lawrie says that his most memorable and saddest moment in soccer was 'playing and losing to

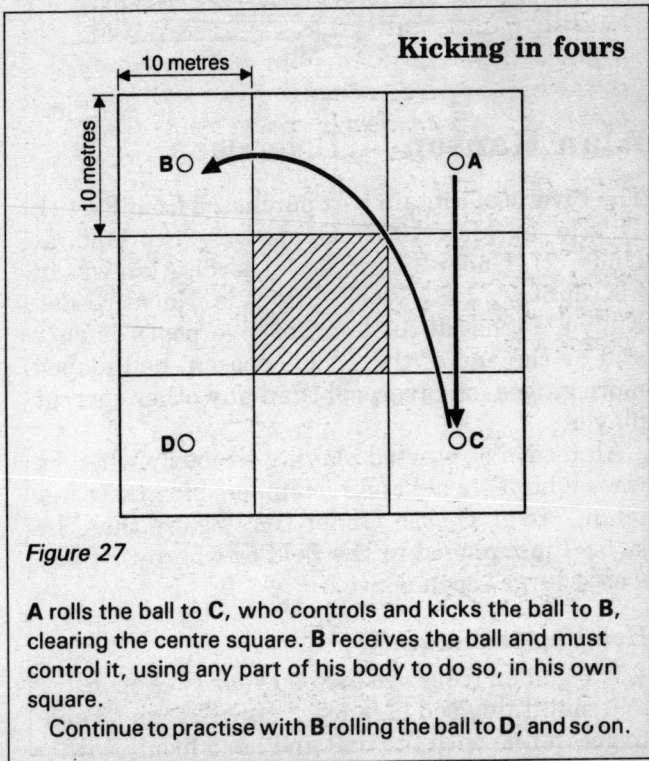

Kicking in fours

Figure 27

A rolls the ball to C, who controls and kicks the ball to B, clearing the centre square. B receives the ball and must control it, using any part of his body to do so, in his own square.

Continue to practise with B rolling the ball to D, and so on.

Everton in the FA Cup semi-final in 1985'. He advises youngsters to 'be confident in your own ability, yet be prepared to take advice because other people's experiences are vital to your own learning'.

Alan Hansen – Defender

The Liverpool captain was purchased from Partick Thistle in May 1977. Capped by Scotland at Under-21, Under-23 and senior level, Alan was in his country's 1982 World Cup side. He succeeded Emlyn Hughes at the heart of Liverpool's defence and by the end of the 1986/7 season, had played more games for Liverpool than any other current player.

Alan says he started playing seriously when he was eight years old and remembers his first soccer team, Troon Thistle Under-10s. 'Before that,' he says, 'I just played in the field or wherever there was a large, open space.'

Heading technique
❡ The golden rules are to keep your eyes open and maintain good balance. You will then be able to get in line with the ball and head firmly with

the forehead. Keep the neck, back and trunk in a very solid, straight line. Know where you want to head the ball before it gets to you. Controlled headers are those where you look around as the ball is coming, see a player and nod the ball to him. When heading for distance, watch the ball carefully. Distance heading is achieved by using the power of the legs and the back, and by 'pushing' at the ball with the forehead. **'**

Control with the head
' The following technique can be very effective. Bend the knees forming a type of spring, then as the ball makes contact with the head, collapse the knees, taking the weight off the ball. The ball will drop at your feet and you can then take it in any direction. Practise this technique with a partner. **'**

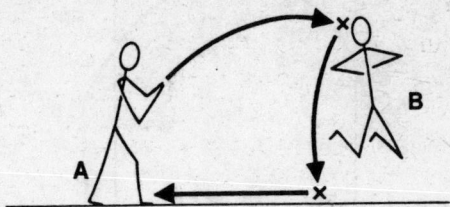

Figure 28

A throws to **B**, who controls the ball with his head. As the ball drops to the feet of **B**, it is passed back to **A**. After ten consecutive headers, **B** serves the ball to **A**.

Steve Williams – Midfield

Steve joined Southampton straight from school and succeeded the famous England dynamo Alan Ball as captain. Steve rose to England international rank himself before joining the Gunners in 1984. Alan Ball is Steve's favourite player of all time because of his great passion for the game.

Steve's advice is for youngsters 'to want to be the best, with the best, at the best'.

The 'chip'

❝ The 'chip' is a technique which is used to get the ball into the air quickly. You have to chop down behind the ball, rather like an axe movement, making contact on the way down, so that back-spin is applied. This makes the ball

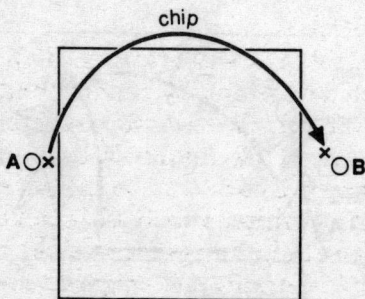

Figure 29

Attempt to clear the space with a 'chip'. Practise in pairs — each player standing on opposite sides of a 10-metre square.

rise quickly. It is the sort of pass you might play over a defender, for a winger to run on when there isn't much room between the full-back and the dead-ball line.

Try to use a 'chip' during a soccer match. Remember at all times to play naturally and with enthusiasm. **❯**

Craig Johnson – Midfield

A South African by birth, Craig joined the staff at Ayresome Park after seeing Middlesbrough FC on a tour of Australia, where he was brought up and where his family lives. By the spring of 1981 he had gained an England Under-21 cap. Craig signed for Liverpool in the same year for £150,000, breaking through to the first team during the 1981/2 season. He played his part in Liverpool's FA Cup triumph of 1986, by scoring a goal.

Chest control

❮ Chest control involves letting the ball hit the body in such a way that, by bending and turning to the right or left, the ball drops off at an angle and under control. Remember to keep the arms out of the way to avoid hand ball. Your chest should form a cushion, which will then absorb the pace of the ball. You can 'chest' the ball down to your own feet or direct it upwards, and then volley the ball. You can even pass the ball off your chest by deflecting it to a team-mate.

When practising control with the chest, serve or kick the ball into the air towards your partner, so that it can be taken before it bounces. Most importantly, keep practising, no matter what! **❯**

Gary Stevens – Midfield

An apprentice with Brighton, with whom he starred in the 1983 FA Cup Finals, Gary was capped at England Under-21 level before moving to Spurs in 1983 for £350,000. He is now an established full international, having appeared for England in the 1986 World Cup finals in Mexico. A true partriot, Gary recalls crying when England lost to Poland at Wembley and when they failed to qualify for earlier finals.

Gary stresses the importance of practising basic skills of passing and control.

Passing

❛ Most passes are made while the ball is actually moving or while it is being brought under control. In order to pass you first need to control the ball. One very important factor in passing is the weighting of the ball according to how fast the ball must travel. A player who is moving will probably need the ball about 5–10 metres in front of him, and it is important that the pass coincides with the run being made. Remember to look around before deciding what to do, but don't let opponents come close enough to obstruct the pass.

You can practise the technique of passing in a 10-metre grid (Figure 30). This will give you plenty of time to control the ball and look around before you are put under real pressure. **’**

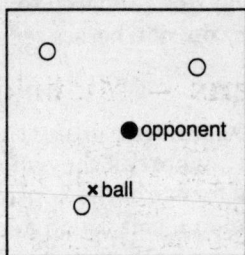

Figure 30

Play in teams of three, with one opponent, in a 10-metre square.

‘ Small-sided team games are also a great help – anything form 2 v 2 to 7 v 7. Remember to support the player with the ball. It isn't always possible to play the ball forwards. You can turn out of a tight situation and lay the ball back to someone who is on your team who is supporting. He may be in better position than you to deliver an accurate pass elsewhere. **’**

Paul Davis – Midfield

Born in Stockwell, south London, on 9 December 1961, Paul joined Arsenal after a schoolboy career with South London Boys. He developed in the Gunners' apprentice ranks, and made his League debut for the side against Spurs in April 1980, aged eighteen. A key member of the victorious Littlewoods Cup-winning side in 1987, Paul is recognized as one of the most gifted midfield players in the First Division. He has also won England Under-21 honours.

Paul says: 'Always be prepared to look, listen and learn. Above all, do not be scared to fail.'

Control

❝ Most players, when controlling the ball, tend to stand and wait, whereas they should be encouraged to go forward and control as quickly as possible. Develop a soft touch and learn to take the pace off the ball, with whatever part of the body is in line with the ball.

Control the ball with your legs. If a ball is coming out of the air, control it with the thigh so that it drops in front of you; then nudge it in the direction you want to go. If you want to go to the right, let the ball hit the thigh and, as it does so, bring the leg away, giving slightly, to get the soft control. At the same time, lean so that the ball comes off in the right direction. Throw the ball in the air, chase and control it, guiding it quickly to the right or left. ❞

When Len Shackleton, of Sunderland and England fame, was playing against a continental team, an opposing player tugged at his shorts every time he went for the ball. 'Shack' removed his shorts and handed them to his opponent, saying, 'There you are; if you like them that much, keep them.'

Jesper Olsen – Striker

Danish-born Jesper began his career in his home land with Naesteved, but made his name after moving to Holland and signing for Ajax. Manchester United brought him to England for a fee of £350,000 in April 1984. He was one of the stars of Denmark's glittering World Cup team in Mexico 1986.

'Work hard in training,' says Jesper, 'and keep believing in your own ability.'

Dribbling

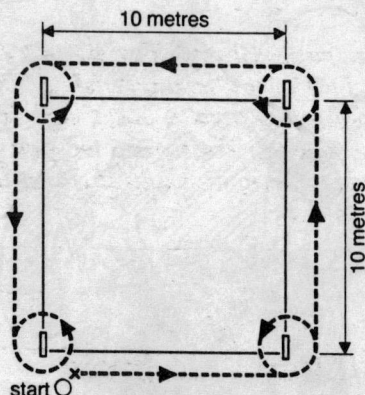

Figure 31

Place one skittle at each corner of a 10-metre square. Dribble the ball around the square. At the first skittle, dribble round it with the inside of one foot only; at the second skittle use the outside of the foot only, and so on, using the inside and outside of the foot alternately, and changing feet.

It's a funny game

Bill Shankly always joined the Liverpool players in the six-a-side match which ended the day's training. He hated losing, and on one occasion, with scores level, there was dispute about a goal 'scored' against his side. There was doubt about the ball having crossed the line between the two posts, and since it would have been the winning goal, 'Shanks' was protesting loudly. Only the Liverpool manager felt the ball had not gone in, but he insisted on letting the quiet man of Anfield, Chris Lawlor, the nearest to the incident, decide the outcome.

'Tell the truth, Chris, your honest opinion. Was the ball over the line?' asked Shanks.

'It was definitely a goal, boss,' replied Chris. Shanks exploded: 'I've waited ten years for the man to open his mouth and the first thing he tells me is a lie!'

Paul McStay – Midfield

Midfield star Paul has already collected Scottish Championship, Cup and League Cup winners' medals during his short but spectacular career at Celtic. When he made his senior international debut against Uruguay more than four years ago, he became the second youngest international in Scottish history. Only Denis Law got his call-up at an earlier age.

The 'wall' pass

Figure 32

A moves towards the defender, **Y**, threatening to dribble past him to the right. In the meantime, player **B** has taken up a position where he can, for a moment, stand still facing his team-mate. It is easy for **A** to pass to him. When the pass is given, **B** gives a first-time return pass behind the opponent, which **A** can take in his stride. **A** is 'bouncing' the ball off **B**, who acts as a 'wall'.

This is commonly used in football, to get behind an opponent in two passes.

Overlap run

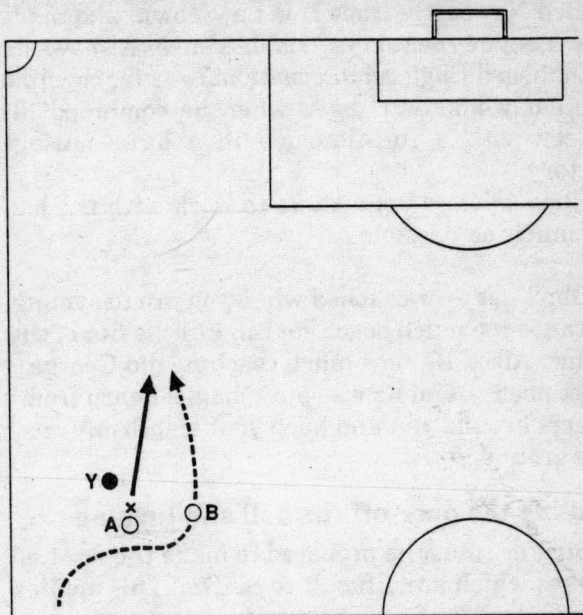

Figure 33

In the same situation, **B** might run behind **A**. **B** has run into position for a 'wall' pass, but the opposing player, **Y**, has positioned himself to stop it. Continuing his run, **B** moves behind **A** and then sends his run in a forward direction, at which time **A** pushes the pass beyond the defender.

Chris Waddle – Striker

Tottenham paid £590,000 to sign Chris from Newcastle United during the summer of 1985. He joined Newcastle from Tow Law Town, and made his League debut in 1980. Chris is now an established England international – a far cry from his early amateur days, when he combined his soccer with a full-time job in a local sausage factory.

Chris advises youngsters to work with the ball as much as possible.

‘ Don't get over-coached when you are too young, because too much coaching can kill the fun of the game. After all, how much coaching did George Best need – and he was pure magic! Learn from others around you and keep your feet firmly on the ground. ’

Taking the pace off the ball and turning

‘ Strikers must be prepared to make the most of passes which are difficult to control. This applies particularly to central strikers or centre-forwards. On many occasions they will be challenged strongly while receiving the ball and when they are facing the wrong way – their backs pointing towards the opposing goal.

An important skill involves 'laying-off' passes to other players who are in a better position to go forward. Whenever he is given the smallest amount of space, however, the striker should be able to control the ball and turn to face his opponent in the same movement. ’

Cyrille Regis – Striker

West Bromwich Albion signed Cyrille from Isthmian League club Hayes Town in 1977. He later moved to Coventry City. The biggest disappointment in Cyrille's career was when he pulled his right hamstring and was unavailable for the 1982 World Cup finals.

Half volleys and volleys

' A half volley is when you strike the ball at the moment it hits the ground. It is difficult to control the direction and height of a half volley. The timing must be perfect. You must keep your knee and head over the ball so that it travels low and straight.

A full volley (or volley) is when the ball is struck in mid-air. The volley is a stabbing action with very little follow-through and, by keeping head and knee over the ball, it can be kept low. '

It's a funny game

Mark Lawrenson: When I was waiting for a stretcher to carry me off injured when playing for Brighton, the two ambulancemen carrying the stretcher fell over.

Brian McClair – Striker

Brian started his career for Motherwell, and after joining Celtic he was the top scorer for four seasons before joining Manchester United in the summer of 1987. His most memorable achievement to date was winning the Premier League title with Celtic in 1986.

As Brian says: 'One of the most important skills to learn is keeping the ball up in the air, which forms a part of one of the most important assets of the game: control of the ball.'

Control

❝ Using only feet, legs, chest and head, keep the ball up for three successive bounces, then play the ball to a partner. Repeat the sequence of three successive bounces, then play the ball back to your partner. After being passed back by your partner, the ball may be allowed to bounce once on the ground. Try to achieve as many sequences in succession as possible, and remember to stay within a 10-metre square. ❞

Kevin McAllister – Striker

Kevin, Chelsea's Scottish signing, was top scorer for Falkirk, the Scottish League Division One team in the 1983/4 season. His most prized possessions are his Falkirk 'Young Player of the Year' trophy and his Scottish Junior Cup.

Kevin encourages youngsters to 'keep your heads up and don't lose heart when things don't go right.'

Figure 34

GK

●defender
forward Ǒ

1

GK

● defender
Ǒ ○ forward

2

Practise with goals and a goalkeeper, one against one, and insist that one player take the other on in order to get a shot under pressure (see illustration 1).

You can also practise in a two against two situation, again with a target (see illustration 2).

Dribbling with aggression

❬ This is increasing the pace of the dribbling, and running with the ball. First control the ball, then accelerate; don't run flat out but at three-quarter speed, leaving room for acceleration when challenged. You can slow down and accelerate, or change direction and accelerate. When you attack a defender at speed, he will attempt to match your speed. This is where you need aggression and purpose to get the ball past him. Remember not to let the ball get too far away or too close to the opponent. The ball must be far enough in front to tempt him, but close enough to ensure that if he makes the tackle you can knock the ball past him. ❭

Michael Glynn – Striker

Michael played 152 games for Peterborough, his home-town club, before signing for Coventry City, in unusual circumstances, in August 1983. Coventry's manager, Bobby Gould, happened to be watching from his office window when Michael scored twice in a pre-season friendly.

Dribbling

❬ Dribbling is running with the ball but not letting the ball get too far away. Control the ball with your better foot, inside and out, taking it where you want to go. Don't look down at the ball – you must know where others are coming from, so look up all the time.

When taking the ball up to a player, control it with the inside or outside of a foot, so that you can change direction quickly, catching him off balance. Take a ball to a player using the inside of a foot, threatening to accelerate to the left. Then, by stopping the ball and using the outside of the foot, changing direction quickly, you will probably throw him off balance enough to get by him on his left.

Use of the body to throw opponents off balance is very important. Swing the body to the left and right when controlling the ball. This will help to confuse the opponent. When learning to dribble, you must develop a 'feel' for the ball. 〞

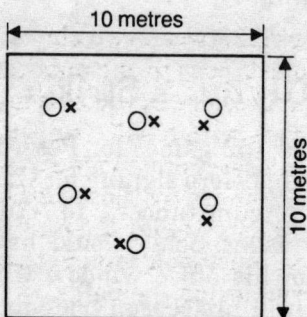

Figure 35

Give each player a ball inside a 10-metre square. Use as many players as you like and ask them to dribble the ball, using the sole, the outside or the inside of the foot, but trying to avoid each other. Make a game of it; keep your own ball and at the same time try to knock someone else's ball out of the square. The winner is the last remaining player still in possession of his ball.

Jim Beglin – Defender

Born in Waterford, Jim played for Shamrock Rovers before signing for Liverpool. He suggests three separate exercises to develop ball control.

Dribbling

i) Run with the ball anywhere in the playing area and get a 'feel' for the ball – imagine the ball is tied to your feet with elastic that won't stretch for more than one metre. Use the outside as well as the inside of the foot.

Look around you while you keep control. Soccer is a team game and you must be aware of the movements of players around you.

ii) Use one ball between two players, 5–10 metres apart; pass to one another while running anywhere in the playing area.

iii) Four players with a ball, two without. Players in possession move anywhere, but can be challenged by those without the ball. This ensures that the players in possession must look around them if they are to avoid losing the ball.

You can also practise 'shielding', which means keeping the body between the challenger and the ball – an important aspect of control.

It's a funny game

David Speedie – Striker

Now with Coventry, the Scottish striker was originally spotted by a Barnsley scout, playing football in Doncaster. David's most memorable moments were making his debut for Scotland and also scoring a hat-trick in a Cup Final at Wembley for Coventry City. He was very disappointed at being left out of the Scottish World Cup Squad for Mexico.

David stresses the importance of good calling during team play.

Calling instructions

❬ Calling instructions during practice and in team play is as important as any other skill in the game and, like everything else, it must be practised.

Here are a few simple instructions that can be repeated many times during a practice.

Hold – this call should be made by the passer to the player receiving the ball if the opponent is some distance away and not, therefore, likely to make a tackle. The receiver may be fully aware that the opponent is not within tackling distance, but there are occasions when he isn't and he must rely upon such a call.

Pass – this call is appropriate when a player receives a ball under pressure from an opponent, and hasn't time or space to bring the ball under control.

Asking for a pass – this call should be made when the caller is moving into a position where he can be reached by a simple pass – for example, when he is in a supporting position to the player in possession. Get into the habit of calling the name of the player in possession.

Remember – all calls must be simple and have a clear purpose. ❜

It's a funny game

Keith Houchen: *I got stuck under an advertising board at Fratton Park during a Portsmouth v Coventry game. That was bad enough, but an irate Pompey fan then started hitting me with a brolly.*

Allan Evans – Defender

Allan was signed as a schoolboy by Scottish club Dunfermline, who transferred him to Aston Villa. He is a Scottish international.

Allan recommends small-sided games to improve a youngster's natural ability and allow it to develop.

Dribbling

' Small-sided games in 10-metre squares are good for dribbling practice because players are put under pressure. If players hold the ball for a few seconds, this will encourage dribbling and, at the same time, make them aware that someone is trying to take the ball away from them. It also makes the point that all you can do is control and dribble the ball until you get support.

Add this rule to the game: the player on the ball must find and pass to the player farthest away from him. This gives the player taking the pass more time to control the ball and opens the game, preventing crowding in corners of the pitch. Now the player in possession must go towards an opponent and beat him before making a pass. '

Tony Adams – Defender

Born in Romford on 10 October 1966, Tony was a member of Arsenal's Littlewoods Cup-winning team in 1987. Tony won the Professional Footballers' Association 'Young Player of the Year' award in the same year.

Control

6 Using the inside of the foot to take the pace off the ball rolling along the ground, practice these ball-control exercises.

i) Use one ball between two players, standing 10 metres apart. Pass the ball with the inside of the foot firmly to each other. Control it with the inside of the foot, and return it along the ground. The person receiving the ball must offer a foot to the approaching ball, and withdraw it as soon as the ball makes contact with the inside of the foot. Withdrawal of the relaxed leg and foot takes the pace off the ball.

The players now pass the ball to each other as they move, control it with the inside of the foot, move off with it under control and return it when they see the opportunity.

ii) Play four against one in a 10-metre square. The single player tries to intercept as the other four practise passing and controlling the ball between them. 9

> **Rob Johnson:** *A young professional, in all seriousness, told me to get the crosses in from one side, because the sun would be in our eyes if we crossed from the other.*

Steve Clarke – Defender

Chelsea paid St Mirren £400,000 for Steve, a Scottish Under-21 international.

Tackling

❛ A tackle is used when a player, with the ball under close control, moves directly at the challenger who, in order to make a successful challenge, blocks the movement of the ball with the inside of the tackling foot.

In an exercise to develop tackling skills, the ball is placed on the ground between two players so that each needs to make one stride to challenge for it. At a signal from another player they each take a stride forward and block the ball with the inside of the same foot.

Coaching points

Make sure that the main tackling foot is placed firmly on the ground alongside the ball with toe pointing forward. The body should be leaning forward, so that the player is looking down at the ball. The inside of the foot should be presented to the ball, as if making a pass with the inside of the foot. ❜

Doug Rougvie – Defender

Born in Fife, Doug Rougvie moved from Aberdeen to Chelsea for a fee of £50,000. He later moved to Brighton.

Doug suggests a couple of practice exercises to improve tackling techniques.

Tackling

❝ i) Use one ball between two players. One player dribbles the ball, closely under control, directly towards his partner, who tries to make a successful tackle. The player winning the ball then dribbles towards his dispossessed partner, who becomes the challenger.

ii) Use a similar formation as for the previous practice, but now the person with the ball has a target. The object is to reach a line 20 metres away without being tackled. If the challenger wins the ball, he takes it back to the line from which the other started, and the practice continues with roles reversed. ❞

Martin Foyle – Striker

Southampton signed Salisbury-born Martin for a one-year apprenticeship, having spotted him playing local football. Martin moved to Aldershot for £10,000, later joining Oxford in a £140,000 deal.

'Don't worry about making mistakes,' advises Martin.

Losing your marker

❝ Man-for-man marking is a battle of wits between you and your marker. The defender will probably stand one side of you, between you and the goal. This is to try to force you wide, away from your target, but it will also allow you to be in front and get the ball.

Tell your fellow players to pass to the foot farther from your defender, giving you the chance to run wide and cut back in. By turning away from your marker you keep your body between him and the ball, which gives you the advantage. Once you have the ball, you can turn and run at him quickly. **❞**

It's a funny game

A professional footballer, well known for his lack of respect towards referees, approached one official and asked, 'What would you do if I called you an idiot?'
'I'd have to send you off,' came the reply.
'Well, what would you do if I thought you were an idiot?'
'If you only thought it, I couldn't send you off, could I?' explained the ref.
'Well, I think you're an idiot.'

Dean Saunders – Striker

Swansea-born Dean played for his home-town club before moving to Oxford via Brighton.

'Train hard and play your own game,' says Dean.

Skill practice

❝ Many goals are scored from within the 6-yard box, the area of the field closest to the goals in which the striker must remain ice-cool and yet ever alert for a shooting opportunity. Whereas from longer distances you should aim low, aim for the roof of the net once in the 6-yard box. This is because defenders and goalkeepers will come at you low and your shot has to be high enough to rise above them. ❞

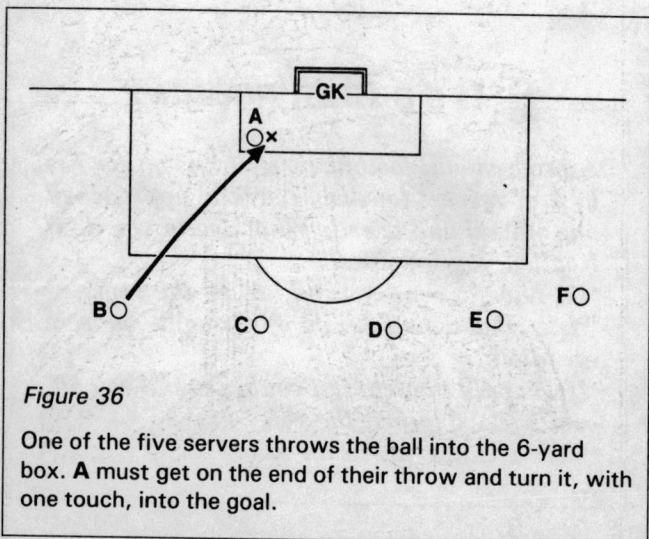

Figure 36

One of the five servers throws the ball into the 6-yard box. **A** must get on the end of their throw and turn it, with one touch, into the goal.

It's a funny game

Peter Davenport: *Last season I was left behind when the team bus departed for Coventry. I managed to get to the ground before them by hitching a lift, but the funny thing was that nobody had realized I was missing.*

It's a funny game

BBC sports commentator Tony Gubba was sitting in the directors' lounge with his counterpart, Brian Moore of ITV, just before the Cup Final between Coventry and Spurs. A fan, walking past, came up to Tony and asked, 'John Motson, can I have your autograph?' Brian Moore laughed, at which the man turned to Brian and said, 'Don't worry, Barry, you can sign in a minute.'

Neil MacDonald – Defender/Midfield

A product of Wallsend Boy's Club, where Newcastle United's youth development officer was his main influence, Neil played for England Schoolboys and has also been capped at Under-21 level. He came to Newcastle United after a short spell with Carlisle.

Neil advises youngsters to enjoy what they do and remember that 'you don't have to win to be good'. One of the best crossers of the ball in the First Division, Neil recommends that youngsters practise this technique.

Skill practice

❛ Much attacking play can be wasted if the final pass is not accurate. In this activity, the player is given the task of centring the ball from various wing positions, to other players. He receives service of the ball from another player and then practises the following:

- lobs to the far post after fast run to the corner;
- runs towards penalty area and passes on ground or makes a short chip;
- runs down the right wing and checks, and centres with left foot;
- low, fast drives out of goalkeeper's reach;
- running with ball and chipping over advancing goalkeeper. *

David Cooper – Striker

Born into a footballing family at Hamilton, Avondale, on 25 February 1956, David stayed in Scotland, moving from Clydebank to Glasgow Rangers in 1977. A Scottish Under-21 and full international, David was groomed for stardom by his manager, Jock Wallace. His saddest moment in soccer was the night in Cardiff when the Scottish team manager Jock Stein died after suffering a heart attack.

David advises youngster to 'always expect things to go wrong and that way you will not be surprised, you will be prepared'.

Wing play

❛ A winger must be able to control the ball skilfully, often in very restricted conditions. When a defender serves the ball to you, he must feel sure that you will not lose possession to the opposing full-back. Whatever the type of service, the winger must learn to control the ball, to take it away from an onrushing defender, or quickly upfield in a sweeping attack. Good skill in controlling the ball will enable the wing-forward to screen the ball from an opponent or make a quick getaway from the spot. **,**

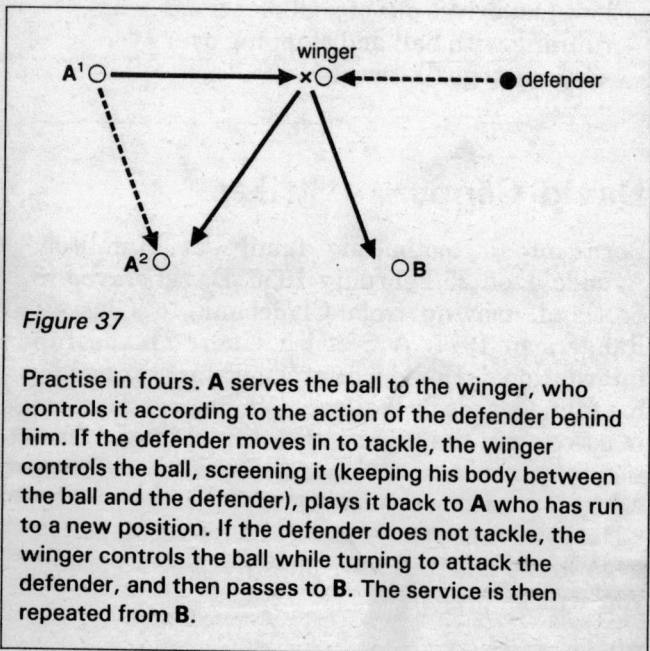

Figure 37

Practise in fours. **A** serves the ball to the winger, who controls it according to the action of the defender behind him. If the defender moves in to tackle, the winger controls the ball, screening it (keeping his body between the ball and the defender), plays it back to **A** who has run to a new position. If the defender does not tackle, the winger controls the ball while turning to attack the defender, and then passes to **B**. The service is then repeated from **B**.

Hans Segers – Goalkeeper

The Dutchman joined Nottingham Forest having played for PSV Eindhoven in his native Holland. Hans' favourite player of all time is Johan Cruyff.

Understanding with defenders

❝ A goalkeeper must have a good understanding with other defenders, especially the centre-backs and the two full-backs, so that each knows what to do. It is useful in practice to produce a sequence of attacking situations similar to those in a game, as in Figure 38. ❞

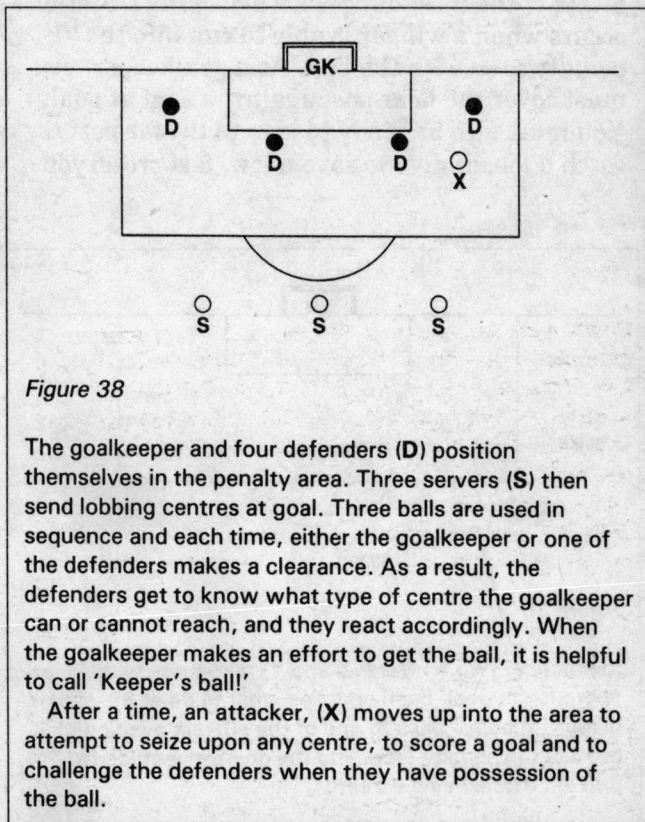

Figure 38

The goalkeeper and four defenders (D) position themselves in the penalty area. Three servers (S) then send lobbing centres at goal. Three balls are used in sequence and each time, either the goalkeeper or one of the defenders makes a clearance. As a result, the defenders get to know what type of centre the goalkeeper can or cannot reach, and they react accordingly. When the goalkeeper makes an effort to get the ball, it is helpful to call 'Keeper's ball!'

After a time, an attacker, (X) moves up into the area to attempt to seize upon any centre, to score a goal and to challenge the defenders when they have possession of the ball.

Peter Hucker – Goalkeeper

Peter's association with Queens Park Rangers started as a schoolboy, although he could have chosen from a host of other clubs. He moved to Oxford in a £100,000 transfer deal. Over six feet tall, Peter is an England Under-21 goalkeeper.

Dealing with an attack from the wing

❢ One of the most dangerous attacking situations occurs when a winger is able to run into the penalty area with the ball. As a goalkeeper, you must cover the near post against a shot at goal. You must also be ready to leap to the far post to catch a lob, or dive to save a low, fast cross; you

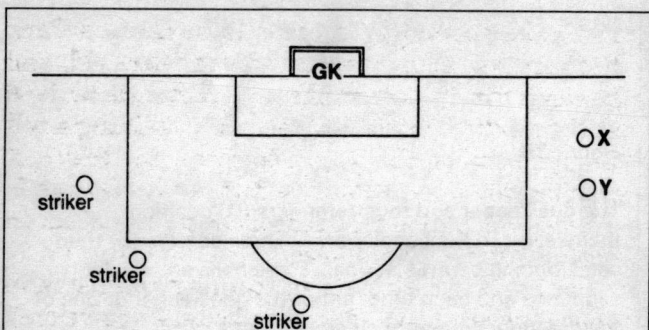

Figure 39

In practice, two wingers (**X** and **Y**) take turns to make an approach at goal. Each chooses what to do at the end of his run, shoot or pass to one of the strikers positioned outside the penalty area, and the goalkeeper tries to prevent a goal being scored.

must also get quickly to the middle of the goal to guard against a shot when the winger passes the ball backwards at an angle. **)**

Peter says: 'Never take football too seriously, because if you lose enjoyment it's not worth doing.'

Paul Goddard – Striker

Paul was spotted by a scout from Queens Park Rangers when he was only eleven years old, and he came through the ranks with them. He arrived at Newcastle United via West Ham, gaining a full England cap on the way. Top scorer in 1986/7, it was largely due to Paul's efforts that Newcastle avoided relegation that season, as he scored seven goals in successive games.

Paul says: 'Work hard in training and listen to your coaches. Look after your body – you've only got one!'

Quick shooting

(A striker must be ready to seize upon any half-chance to get in his shot. He cannot wait for perfect openings. Indeed, some of the greatest goals by strikers have been scored from seemingly hopeless positions. **)**

Figure 40

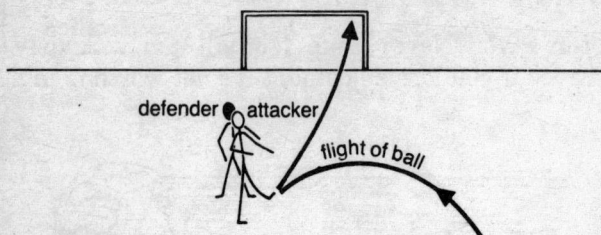

1

The striker is blocked by the defender and the ball arrives at a difficult height, but he is still able to hook the ball on the volley.

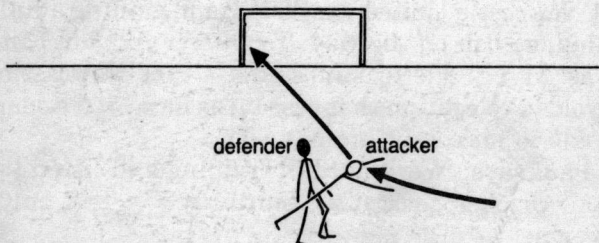

2

In the above situation the striker flings himself forward into a dive so that he reaches the ball before the defender. With his head, he deflects a fast centre into the goal.

It's a funny game

Greg Downs: *Having taken some stick over the years because of my bald head, I decided to wear a wig during the last game of the season against Southampton.*

Kenny Sansom – Full-back

Kenny is one of the finest left-backs in England, having been the country's number one for the past seven seasons. Born in Camberwell, Kenny began his career with Crystal Palace, moving to Highbury in August 1980, and established himself as Arsenal's club captain in 1985. He vividly remembers the game which clinched the Second Division Championship for Palace – a 2–0 win against Burnley in front of a 52,000 crowd.

Full-back tactics

❛ There are times when the attacker approaches with the ball in his possession and a team-mate alongside. This is a two against one situation

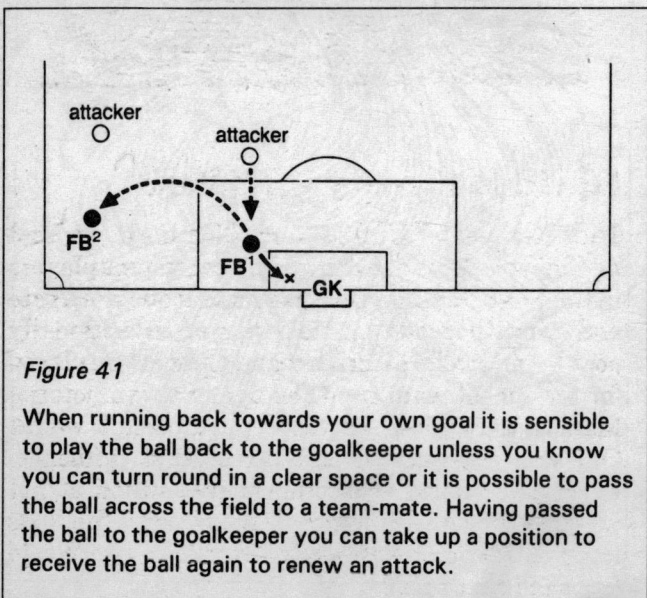

Figure 41

When running back towards your own goal it is sensible to play the ball back to the goalkeeper unless you know you can turn round in a clear space or it is possible to pass the ball across the field to a team-mate. Having passed the ball to the goalkeeper you can take up a position to receive the ball again to renew an attack.

where it would be foolish to dash in to tackle for the ball. As a full-back you must learn how to 'jockey' your opponents' play so that they hesitate. You pretend to go in to tackle and then step back to cut out any hasty pass between the two attackers. Your aim is to force them to delay or to let the ball run loose so that you can pounce on it. You must be nimble on your feet and quick to pivot round from one player to the other. You must feint to tackle in such a way that your opponents are forced to move the ball into a position which gives you the chance to reach it. **"**

David McCreery – Midfield

The Newcastle United and Northern Ireland midfield player is one of the most consistent players in the First Division. David's tremendous work rate and competitive nature make him an exceptionally popular and well-respected team member. He played for his school team from the age of seven, joining Manchester United when he was sixteen. It was at Old Trafford that he met his biggest influence, Tommy Docherty. Although disappointed at not winning an FA Cup Winner's medal with the Reds in 1976, David has played a key role in two World Cups for his country.

Pulling the ball away from a tackle

❛ If an opponent rushes in to tackle, you will find it helpful to use the sole of the foot to pull the ball backwards. You then turn and edge away to work a suitable angle for your next pass. Quick turning movements of this kind will help you to switch attacks from one side of the field to the other. Sometimes when the ball comes towards you at speed you will use the side of the foot to take enough pace from the ball to allow you to turn at the same time. When you are running with the ball you should keep it on the side away from the opponent. You can sell him the dummy by pretending to stop, or by turning round and then darting off in a new direction. ❜

It's a funny game

Tommy Docherty, when manager of Manchester United, held a tough training session a couple of days before a local derby game with City. His centre-forward was Stuart Pearson, who came in apparently complaining of a bad back. Docherty told him, 'Don't worry, son, Manchester City have got two!'

6

A Week in the Life of a Player: Neil Webb

As many of the professionals in this book have remarked, the life of a footballer is not dedicated solely to sheer hard work, essential though it is. Learning to relax properly can be equally important, as well as making time for family life. Neil Webb, who began his career as an apprentice with Reading and now plays for Nottingham Forest, gives an account of a typical week in the life of a professional footballer.

Sunday

This is an unusual Sunday, as we are playing QPR at the City ground. I've still got the leg burn from last week's Guinness six-a-side competition, which Nottingham Forest won. The injury is bothering me a little bit, but it's a great day and we've got a good crowd of over 18,000. By the end of the ninety minutes, Forest have scored four goals including a fantastic Nigel Clough hat-trick in less than five minutes. New boy Tommy Gaynor scored the other.

My current success all seems a far cry from those early days at Reading, particularly one memorable reserve game against Spurs which we lost 9–0, when I played against my hero Glen Hoddle for the first time. I signed for Reading as an apprentice at the age of sixteen, having played for all the Reading schoolboy sides from the Under-11s upwards. My father had played for Reading as a striker for eight years, averaging a goal every two games.

Monday

My fourteen-month-old son, Luke, wakes me and I reluctantly get out of bed. My legs feel like lead – thank goodness we have the day off. I take our two golden retrievers, Rosie and Pumpkin, for a walk in Wollaton Park. It is a crisp, cold day, but we walk for about two miles. I listen to my Walkman to get away from it all. Afterwards, it's back to reality – I have to attend a business meeting and then cook the dinner. It's a good job that I studied for domestic science 'O' Level!

Tuesday

The team has a training session which includes a competitive five-a-side game. We have the usual series of sprint races and I come last, as always – not my strong point. It is important to work hard, listen and learn during training, but also never to lose your love and enthusiasm for the game. Playing football isn't just about skill, it is also about commitment and enjoyment – aspects which can help to improve your play.

Tonight is the chairman's Christmas party. After several glasses of wine, I take to the dance-floor. (Don't worry, my wife Shelley is teetotal, and she drives us home afterwards.)

Wednesday

Another day off – this time to recover from last night's party – it's not always like this, folks! My peace and quiet are shattered, as I am dragged off to do some Christmas shopping by the demon I call my wife.

At tea-time I'm off to a Christmas party – for underprivileged children. This is an area of my work which I really love, the kids are great and they always make me realize that there are more important things in life than football.

When I return home, I watch the television for a while; my favourite programmes are *Cheers* and *The Cosby Show*. Before going to sleep, I read a chapter of *The Godfather*.

It's a funny game

Tommy Docherty, on hearing of Manchester United's bid for Remi Moses, is alleged to have exclaimed: 'Half a million pounds for Remi Moses? You could get the original Moses and the Tablets for that price!'

Thursday

The weather is awful. It's throwing it down, and Shelley complains that she's got to bike it to college. I remind her that I need the car to drop Luke off at the child-minder's, so I smile sympathetically as the door slams. Luke and I are able to have breakfast together before I go training.

This is followed by a quick trip to the dentist — which is essential, because pain puts me off my game — and I don't forget to call in at the local supermarket for the groceries. I prefer a quiet social life, with an occasional game of golf, but this is a busy week and I'm off out again to the Heanor branch of the Nottingham Forest Supporters' Club, who are my kit sponsors.

Friday

After a good training session I learn that there is a piece in the evening newspaper by the boss. He is saying that it would be a great Christmas present if I signed a new contract. The national reporters, football's own rat-pack, are waiting for me in the Jubilee Club. I play a few games of pool and then I try to sneak out unnoticed through the back door. No such luck — they all rush after me, one of them still carrying his dinner. After having fobbed them off with 'No comment', it is back home for my regular helping of canelloni and lasagne before travelling to Oxford. During the coach journey, I play Master Team with some of the lads, followed by a game of Scrabble at the hotel before bedtime.

Saturday

I wake up feeling terrible. I'm taking penicillin for a gum infection and it doesn't agree with me. I go for a walk before setting off for the match. I always like to do well at the Manor Ground, Oxford, as it is near my home-town of Reading. Also, my former manager at Reading, Maurice Evans, is now in charge of Oxford United.

I am reminded of the time when I played for Portsmouth against Oxford in a top-of-division clash a few years ago. That game was held up because a Father Christmas ran on to the pitch – and we then scored two goals in as many minutes during the time added on for stoppage. Today's game is less eventful, but the result is also in our favour as we win 2–0, although we could have had more. Brian Rice and Calvin Plummer scored the goals. I am pleased with my own performance, but annoyed with myself because I lost my temper after getting an elbow in the face.

It is back to Nottingham, where Shelley and I go out for a meal with my best mate, Steve Wigley of Birmingham City, his wife and two other couples. By now, I'm beginning to feel really rough. The heat of the restaurant and the cigarette smoke, which I hate, are taking effect. The arrival of my starter – pasta, as usual – is the last straw. After a visit to the loo, my wife takes me home – what a rotten end to an otherwise great week!

7
The Commercial Side of Soccer

Without the active support of business, many clubs would find it difficult or even impossible to continue in their present form. The money taken at the gate from the paying public is no longer sufficient to run a modern football club. Because of the entertainment value of our national sport, transfer fees are high and the best players demand big wages, and although attendances are improving, they are still lower than they were twenty years ago – so how can the clubs survive?

In recent years, the solution to the problem has rested with sponsorship. At the most basic level, a local firm might provide the match ball, thus leading to one journalist's famous comment: 'The game was so bad that at half-time the sponsors asked for their ball back.' At the other end of the scale, the entire Football League and several cup competitions are under major sponsorship. In addition, television companies pay millions of pounds annually for the privilege of televising live games – some of which finds its way to the League clubs.

Most League clubs have gained sponsorship for the entire team, as witnessed by the sight of player's shirts emblazoned with the name of the company. Other firms might sponsor individual games, or purchase executive boxes where their customers can be entertained. Every club will have a commercial manager to deal with these matters, and this person will probably also have responsibility for lottery schemes, the club shop with its sales of souvenirs in appropriate colours, and the selling of advertising space in the match-day programme.

A typical relationship between one company and a football club is that of Solvite and Watford Football Club. Watford, one of the most positive clubs in the country with a bright family image, offered what was felt to be a superb sales platform for a locally based national business. The company has invested nearly £250,000 in the club over a two-year period. There are clear benefits to the club, not least of which is the entertainment that can thus be provided, which has recently included a balloon race, fund-raising events for a hospital scanner appeal, and free gifts for the fans. In return, the sponsors are guaranteed national exposure on television, thereby receiving relatively cheap advertising coverage.

Probably one of the most unusual sponsorship deals in the history of the game occurred when Newcastle Breweries helped to bring the legendary Kevin Keegan to the home-town club. It was part of the brewery's policy to become more involved in the social life of the area – Newcastle United and their fanatical supporters were an important part of the plan. The signing of Kevin Keegan, which was to transform the club and lead to a return to First Division status, was a fillip for the supporters and also for a North-East hard hit by unemployment. Of course, it led to good trade for the brewery as well!

John Gibson, Sports Editor of the Newcastle *Evening Chronicle*, describes the impact Keegan had when he arrived at St James's Park.

‘The scene was fit for the entrance of an American president. Reporters, hard-bitten with their ‘seen it all before’ attitude, whispered excitedly amongst themselves in anticipation. Radio men fidgeted, making certain that their mikes were plugged in and their tape-recorders capturing every word. Television crews were scurrying everywhere, with the special, nervous energy which makes a live television broadcast.

The time was 6.30 p.m. on 19 August 1982. The place was a private room in the Gosforth Park Hotel on the outskirts of Newcastle. Newcastle United were about to make what they, unashamedly, called, ‘the greatest signing in our history’. They had landed Kevin Keegan against all the odds. Even Russell Cushing, the well-respected general manager, forgot himself a little as he rose to his feet and, borrowing some of

Muhammed Ali's razzmatazz, announced, 'We're in heaven — we've got Kevin.' Keegan swept into the room, confident and smiling as the television commentator's voice shot off at a machine-gun rate. **'**

Newcastle United chairman Stan Seymour and manager Arthur Cox were the inspiration behind a signing which startled the soccer world and left most clubs green with envy. United's trump card was played when they contacted their main sponsors to ask for their full support, the idea being that Newcastle Breweries would top up Kevin's wages substantially in an entirely separate deal, by also signing him to do promotional work.

Reg Corbidge, Sales Director of Newcastle Breweries, explains.

' It was made plain that Kevin, who does not drink beer, would not be pictured with a pint of beer in his hand, and that was fine by us. We were keen to retain his clean-cut image with young people. Instead, we wanted to use his great talent in public relations, to go out and meet his fans. **'**

During his two years on Tyneside, Kevin took part in talk-ins at social clubs and pubs, but of perhaps greater importance were his coaching sessions with local kids. The 'Kevin Keegan Soccer Days' brought hundreds of youngsters to the Newcastle United training ground at Benwell, where they benefited from professional coaching before enjoying sandwiches and lemonade. Reg Corbidge continues:

❝ While it was a genuine, community-based, public relations exercise, my company also benefited from the publicity. I believe that the brewery played its part in encouraging Kevin Keegan to come to Newcastle, but Arthur Cox and Stan Seymour should take most of the credit. Arthur already knew he had a good chance of signing Kevin. ❞

In order to attract the right sponsors, it is important for a club to have a bright image and a good stadium. The recent construction of a four-million-pound stand at St James's Park, Newcastle (to replace the old one, condemned unfit by the City Council) shows recognition of the importance of good facilities for a football club. Many supporters would, however, rather see their money spent on players than ground improvements − so what are the advantages?

For a start, the new stand will house thirty-nine new executive boxes which will bring half a million pounds to the club each season, on top of the extra cash from the 2000 additional seats. In addition, a good ground makes a good impression, attracts television companies and brings more advertisers to the club. Newcastle United know that the new stand will make money, which could then be spent on improving the team. Russell Cushing, their general manager, is confident that the club can now build a team that can aim for the top of the First Division.

The world of commerce can also prevent football clubs which can't make ends meet from going out of business. An example of this occurred in 1986, when Middlesbrough Football Club was in the hands of the Official Receiver – in other words, bankrupt – with no money to pay players' wages and in debt to the tune of £1.9 million. The gates of Ayresome Park were locked, and for a while it looked as if League Football would never be played there again. This would have spelt disaster for the supporters, living in an area already depressed by unemployment.

However, at least one of Middlesbrough's directors was determined that the club should not die. Steve Gibson, a local businessman, contacted other firms in the area including ICI, a major employer in Cleveland, and Newcastle Breweries, who were both willing to help the club. The local council financed a report which showed that Middlesbrough could survive on crowds of 10,000. An advertisement inviting other firms to help save Boro' was placed in a national newspaper, and a lucky break came when a London company, whose boss just happened to be a life-long Boro' fan, offered a cheque for nearly £250,000. This money, together with additional sums pledged by the local companies, saved the football club from folding, and Middlesbrough FC 1986 was born.

It's a funny game

The referee's whistle pierced the barrage of booing after the Birmingham defender had committed a late tackle on an unfortunate home forward. The guilty party looked amazed when the referee called him over for a lecture.
'What's the matter, ref?' he asked.
'That was a very late tackle, son,' came the reply.
'But I got there as fast as I could, ref.'

After this eleventh-hour rescue the new club
played its first home game at neighbouring
Hartlepool United's ground on 23 August 1986 at
6.30 p.m., Ayresome Park remaining closed for a
further week.

Middlesbrough Football Club is now almost
unique in that the main sponsors are also
shareholders – that is they own the club. The
chairman, Colin Henderson of ICI, explains: 'It was
important to the whole community that League
football should continue at Ayresome Park.' Now
the future looks rosy – under new ownership, and
spurred on by the impressive young management
and coaching team of Bruce Rioch and Colin Todd,
the whole club has been reborn, with good facilities
to match the achievements on the field. One more
example of the crucial importance of sponsorship
to football in the 1980s.

8
All-time Greats

If you ask any professional footballer who he thinks has been the greatest soccer player of all time, the most likely answer is simply, 'Pelé'.

At his peak, Pelé was a footballing phenomenon, widely acclaimed as the most accomplished all-round player in the world. His performances across the globe, whether for Santos, Brazil or New York Cosmos, have been witnessed with an awe and appreciation unequalled in the history of the game.

Born in 1940 at Tres Coracoes, Brazil, the son of a professional footballer, Pelé became known to his family as 'Dico', even though his real name is Edson Arantes do Nascimento! He was given the nickname Pelé at school, a name which has no literal meaning in Portuguese.

A natural athlete, he excelled at football and after many notable performances at junior level he joined the Santos Club when he was fifteen. With Santos he scored the first of his career total of 1300 goals. The match was against Corinthians on 7 September 1956. Pelé confirmed his early promise, with a goal on his debut for Brazil in a 2–1 win against Argentina the following year, when he was seventeen years of age.

In the yellow and green shirt of Brazil, Pelé became the scourge of international defences the

135

world over, and played in three World Cup Championships — those of 1958, 1962 and 1970. Although he missed the '62 Final through injury, he scored in each of the other two — twice against Sweden in 1958 and once against Italy in 1970.

At the height of his career, Pelé was the world's highest-paid footballer, and a millionaire. He bowed out of the international scene in 1971 but continued playing club soccer with Santos, the club with which he had achieved the status of a national hero. In 1974 he signed for New York Cosmos, the top North American side. His goal touch travelled well!

His former Brazilian team manager, Saldanha, once said of Pelé: 'If you ask me who was the best full-back in Brazil, I will say Pelé. If you ask me who is the best winger, I would say Pelé. If you ask me who is the best goalkeeper, I would have to say Pelé. He is like no other footballer.'

Pelé himself is convinced that he was blessed with a divine gift. 'I feel my greatest skill is the ability to make something out of nothing. Of course, you need speed and balance of mind and body, but I have something else which God gave me. I see the ball and others think that there is no danger, and in two seconds there is a goal. God made me a footballer and keeps me a footballer.'

Ray Clemence, of Spurs and England fame, has said of him: 'Pelé was not only a great player on the field, but a wonderful ambassador off it.'

But if Pelé must be regarded as the world's greatest-ever player, several of our own current professionals of the game have particular all-time favourites. Their own personal choices are listed below, with the nominating players or managers shown in brackets.

George Best.   He was a truly gifted player who scored dozens of special goals. He had so many strengths in his game – dribbling, shooting and passing – and he was so quick over short distances. (George Shipley)

He had every quality – the most complete player I have ever seen. (Liam O'Kane)

A great entertainer. (Steve Hardwick)

George was so unpredictable on the ball that anything could happen, which made him very exciting and all fans love excitement.
  (Jim Beglin)

Alan Ball.   . . . because of his passion for the game. (Steve Williams)

Alan Hansen.   He is the complete centre-half because of his skill and knowledge of the game. As a centre-half myself, I admire the fact that he has everything.   (Colin Foster)

Johan Cruyff.   The Dutchman had great skills, leadership and total understanding and know-how about the game.   (Jesper Olsen)

Bobby Moore.   He was my childhood hero. I saw him play once, for West Ham at Norwich, when I was a nipper. I won't forget how, every time he received, cut out or controlled the ball, he made himself the time and space on the ball and then passed it to one of his own team via a long or short pass.   (Gary Stevens)

Ossie Ardiles.   As far as I'm concerned, he is the owner of the best and quickest footballing brain around.   (Gary Stevens)

Kenny Dalglish.   He has tremendous ability and is a perfect professional.   (Mark Reid)

Kenny has natural ability and is a proven goal-scorer — a hard-working player, who always gives value for money.   (Allan Evans)

Diego Maradona.   This man has everything — skill, vision and scoring ability, and he is exciting to watch. (David Rocastle)

The legendary ex-Liverpool manager Bill Shankly once told friends that he had taken his wife out for a special treat on their wedding anniversary. They asked how he had spent the evening. 'Oh, I gave her a real night out,' said Bill. 'I took her to see Tranmere Rovers.'

In later years Shankly denied this story, explaining, 'It wasn't my wedding anniversary, it was her birthday. Can you imagine me getting married in the football season?'

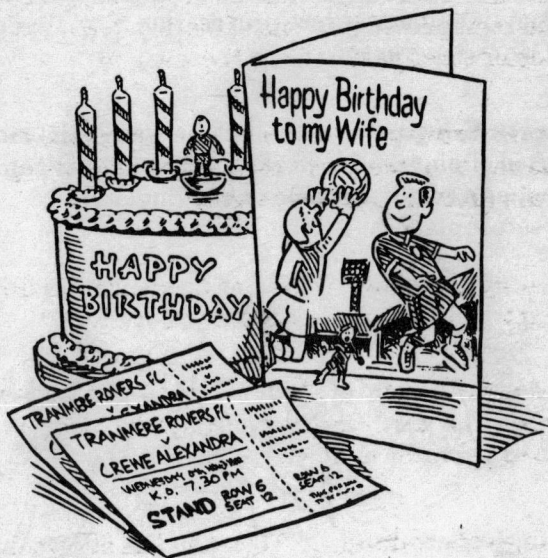

Glen Hoddle.   His ability, like Pelé's, is a gift from God.   (Craig Johnson)

David Webb.   I choose David, of Chelsea and QPR fame, because of his determination and the general ruggedness of his play.   (Cyrille Regis)

Michel Platini.   This Frenchman just doesn't have a weakness in his game.   (David Cooper)

Bobby Charlton.   Bobby had pace, control, balance, passing and shooting ability in both feet. He always possessed a marvellous self-discipline under severe provocation.
  (Mark Lawrenson)

Kevin Keegan.   Although he wasn't the most gifted of players, he worked so hard at his game and, as a result, became one of England's greatest players.   (Robert Lee)

Peter Osgood. Considering Peter was so tall, he had great ball skills and was always good entertainment for the fans. (Greg Downs)

Martin Chivers. This Spurs and England footballer was someone I always admired. (Roy Aitken)

Jimmy Greaves. Quite simply, a goal-scoring legend. I was a striker when I first started playing soccer, and I tried to model myself on his skill, pace and especially his goal-scoring ability. (Steve Gritt)

Ian Rush. Ian Rush is quite simply the striker of the 1980s. He proved this in the 1983/4 season, when he scored 47 goals. That he did it in a side like Liverpool's, full of scoring talent, is another tribute to the Welshman's talent. He is a brilliant one-touch player. I would guess that with 90 per cent of his goals he provides only the finishing strike. He has magnificent timing and speed, enabling him to meet the ball at just the right time and angle. (Malcolm MacDonald)

Pat Jennings. He was the model professional, one of the few people in the game you would want your own kids to be like. A great man and an example for all of us. (Eddie Niedzwiecki)

He was the best – Pat made goalkeeping look easy and he was a gentleman both on and off the pitch.   (Neville Southall)

Steve Heighway.   Steve had the gift of getting to the by-line and crossing the ball perfectly for oncoming strikers.   (Paul Power)

Ian Rush Fact File

Let's end the book with a profile of one of the most successful footballers in the world today

Born in St Asaph, Wales, in October 1961, the ninth of ten children raised by his parents, Doris and Francis. Ian now lives in a two-floored apartment in Turin with his wife Tracey.

Ian turned professional in September 1979 with Chester, and made his League debut on 28 April 1979, wearing the number four shirt, in a 2–2 draw at home to Sheffield Wednesday. He scored his first goal on 15 September 1979, in a 2–2 draw at Gillingham. Liverpool paid Chester £350,000 for Ian in April 1980. He was transferred to Juventus in June 1987, for a staggering £3.2 million. Ian scored 153 goals in 258 football League Games.

A Welsh international, Ian has won practically every honour in the game, collecting League Championship, League Cup, FA Cup and European Cup winners' medals.